SUSAN L. Lingo

MORE

200+

ACTIVITIES

FOR

CHiLDREN'S MiNiSTRY

Standard
PUBLISHING
CINCINNATI, OHIO

Dedication

Show me your ways, O Lord, teach me your paths;
guide me in your truth and teach me.
Psalm 25:4, 5

More 200+ Activities for Children's Ministry

© 2003 Susan L. Lingo

Published by Standard Publishing, Cincinnati, Ohio 45231. A division of Standex International Corporation.

Credits

Produced by Susan L. Lingo, Bright Ideas Books™
Illustrated by Liz Howe
Cover design by Liz Howe

09 08 07 06 05 04   7 6 5 4 3 2
ISBN 0-7847-1315-4
Printed in the United States of America

CONTENTS

Route 52 Road Map

Year 1 | **Year 2**

Ages 3, 4

DISCOVER GOD'S LOVE (42071)

- God Is Great
- God Is Love
- God Is Good
- God Sends His Son, Jesus
- God's Son, Jesus, Grows Up
- God's Son, Jesus
- We Can Know Jesus Is Our Friend
- We Can Know Jesus Is Close to Us
- We Can Be Jesus' Helpers
- We Can Learn to Help
- We Can Learn to Share
- We Can Learn to Love God

DISCOVER GOD'S WORD (42075)

- God Makes the World
- God Makes People
- God Cares for Me
- Jesus Is Born
- Jesus Is God's Son
- Jesus Loves Us
- Being Thankful
- Helping Jesus
- Learning About Me
- Learning from the Bible
- Talking to God
- Helping Others

Ages 4-6

EXPLORE BIBLE PEOPLE (42072)

- Learning That I Am Special (Joseph)
- Learning to Trust God (Gideon)
- Learning to Do What Is Right (Nehemiah)
- Learning to Be Brave (Esther)
- Learning to Pray Always (Daniel)
- Learning to Obey God (Jonah)
- Learning to Love People
- Learning to Be Happy
- Learning to Be Thankful
- Learning to Share
- Learning to Help Others
- Learning to Follow Jesus

EXPLORE BIBLE STORIES (42076)

- Learning About God's Creation
- Learning That God Keeps His Promises
- Learning About God's Care
- Learning About Baby Jesus
- Learning to Be a Friend Like Jesus
- Learning to Follow Jesus
- Learning About Jesus' Power
- Learning That Jesus Is the Son of God
- Learning About the Church
- Learning to Do Right
- Learning That God Is Powerful
- Learning That God Hears My Prayers

Ages 6-8

FOLLOW THE BIBLE (42073)

- The Bible Helps Me Worship God
- The Bible Teaches That God Helps People
- The Bible Helps Me Obey God
- The Bible Teaches That God Answers Prayer
- The Bible Teaches That Jesus Is the Son of God
- The Bible Teaches That Jesus Does Great Things
- The Bible Helps Me Obey Jesus
- The Bible Tells How Jesus Helped People
- The Bible Teaches Me to Tell About Jesus
- The Bible Tells How Jesus' Church Helps People

FOLLOW JESUS (42077)

- Jesus' Birth Helps Me Worship
- Jesus Was a Child Just Like Me
- Jesus Wants Me to Follow Him
- Jesus Teaches Me to Have His Attitude
- Jesus' Stories Help Me Follow Him
- Jesus Helps Me Worship
- Jesus Helps Me Be a Friend
- Jesus Helps Me Bring Friends to Him
- Jesus Helps Me Love My Family
- Jesus' Power Helps Me Worship Him
- Jesus' Miracles Help Me Tell About Him
- Jesus' Resurrection Is Good News for Me to Tell

Ages 8-12

GROW THROUGH THE BIBLE (42074)

- God's Word
- God's World
- God's Chosen People
- God's Great Nation
- The Promised Land
- The Kings of Israel
- The Kingdom Divided, Conquered
- From Jesus' Birth to His Baptism
- Jesus, the Lord
- Jesus, the Savior
- The Church Begins
- The Church Grows
- Reviewing God's Plan for His People

STUDY GOD'S PLAN (42078)

- The Bible Teaches Us How to Please God
- Books of Law Tell Us How God's People Were Led
- History and Poetry Tell About Choices God's People Made
- Prophets Reveal That God Does What He Says
- God Planned. Promised, and Provided Salvation
- Gospels Teach Us What Jesus Did
- Gospels Teach Us What Jesus Said
- Gospels Teach Us That Jesus Is Our Savior
- Acts Records How the Church Began and Grew
- Letters Instruct the Church in Right Living
- OT People and Events Prepare for God's Plan
- NT People and Events Spread God's Plan

Ages 8-12

GROW UP IN CHRIST (42080)

- Growing in Faith
- Growing in Obedience
- Growing in Attitude
- Growing in Worship
- Growing in Discipleship
- Growing in Prayer
- Growing in Goodness
- Growing in Love for Christ
- Growing in Devotion to the Church
- Growing in Grace
- Growing in Confidence
- Growing in Hope

STUDY JESUS' TEACHINGS (42079)

- Jesus Teaches Us About Who God Is
- Jesus Teaches Us that God Loves Us
- Jesus Teaches Us How to Love God
- Jesus Teaches Us About Himself
- Jesus Teaches Us to Do God's Will
- Jesus Teaches Us to Love Others
- Jesus Teaches Us About God's Kingdom
- Jesus Teaches Us How to Live Right
- Jesus Teaches Us the Truth
- Jesus Teaches Us About Forgiveness
- Jesus Teaches Us About God's Power
- Jesus Teaches Us About God's Word

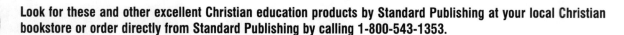

Look for these and other excellent Christian education products by Standard Publishing at your local Christian bookstore or order directly from Standard Publishing by calling 1-800-543-1353.

Standard
PUBLISHING

INTRODUCTION

What happens when you can't enough of something wonderful?

You ask for

Someone once said, "You can't get enough of a good thing," and when it comes to classroom ideas, nothing is more true! Teachers and kids' leaders from every walk of life have used and loved the ideas in the original *200+ Activities for Children's Ministry,* and now they've asked for even *more—more* Bible lessons; *more* creative craft ideas; *more* games; *more* devotions, snacks, and prayers; and even *more* tips, hints, and awesome ideas for classroom management and substitute teachers! In *More 200+ Activities for Children's Ministry* you'll discover over two hundred can't-miss ideas, lively lesson-boosters, snappy activities, and organizational helps divided into eight sections:

- *More* **Creative Crafts**

- *More* **Great Games**

- *More* **Goodies Galore**

- *More* **Prayer & Worship**

- *More* **Devotions & Object Lessons**

- *More* **Super Seasonals**

- *More* **Awesome Organization**

- *More* **SOS for the Substitute**

Each section is loaded with fresh ideas that are as fun for kids as they are friendly for teachers. And scattered throughout every section you'll discover loads of Whatcha Know! boxes that contain helpful hints, ingenious insights, and terrific teaching tips. In addition, each section of *More 200+ Activities for Children's Ministry* has its own mini introduction to provide an overview and solid backdrop for what to expect in the section.

Crafts and games, worship ideas, lively devotions, snacks, and classroom checklists—you'll find them all in *More 200+ Activities for Children's Ministry.* This is the definitive teacher handbook of help, the one book you'll turn to over and over for every classroom concern, each classroom nook and need. There's even a color-coded retrieval system (see page 6) to help you find just the section you're searching for in a snap! You wanted more of a great thing, and here it is: *More 200+ Activities for Children's Ministry!* (Be sure and look for the original *200+ Activities for Children's Ministry* for oodles of ideas aimed at every aspect of your classroom!)

How to Use the Color-Coded Retrieval Tabs

More 200+ Activities for Children's Ministry makes finding your favorite sections of the book as easy as 1-2-3!

1. Photocopy on cardstock the set of tabs below.

2. Color each tab a different color, then cut the tabs out.

3. Tape the tabs to the edges of the corresponding section title pages in a staggered pattern like dividers in a notebook.

| CRAFTS | GAMES | GOODIES | PRAYER & WORSHIP |
| DEVOTIONS | SEASONAL IDEAS | ORGANIZATION TIPS | SOS for the SUBSTITUTE |

MORE CREATIVE CRAFTS

Clever coasters, secret stone hideaways, luscious lip balm, and much more to delight and stretch kids' imaginations!

A Bit of Background

Crafts aren't just enrichment fun—they're creative reinforcement!

Did you realize there's awesome lesson power in providing cool crafts for kids? Arts and crafts projects help lock in learning when they match themes being taught. They provide kids with nonthreatening ways to express themselves and their love for God. Crafts can turn an otherwise dull lesson into an unforgettable adventure. And the best part? Kids have built-in, concrete lesson reminders to carry home and share with their families and friends! Whether you enjoy crafts because of their creative reinforcement, expressive outlets, or enrichment fun, you'll love the creative crafts in *MORE 200+ Activities for Children's Ministry!* And don't be worried about how your kids' projects will turn out, because these no-fail craft ideas are *process-oriented* rather than *product-oriented.* In other words, kids have the creative freedom of expression they need and love!

Consider making a craft cache to keep in your classroom. Collect the following items and keep them in a festive box or basket so you can offer cool craft projects at a moment's notice.

- ☐ markers, crayons, and pencils
- ☐ scissors
- ☐ glue and clear tape
- ☐ paper plates and cups

- ☐ paper lunch sacks
- ☐ ribbon, lace, and trim
- ☐ yarn, string, and twine
- ☐ sequins and glitter

Now here are a few terrific tips to get you started!

✂ **Always plan your crafts ahead of time to be sure you've collected all the materials that will be needed. Make a sample if possible.**

✂ **After messy crafts, let kids "finger paint" with shaving cream on tables—they'll clean up in a snap and make creative cleaning fun!**

✂ **Wash out roll-on deodorant bottles and fill them with liquid tempera paints. Just pop out the roller ball and replace it after filling. Kids love painting with these bodacious bottles!**

PLEASIN' PLATTERS

Nifty plates 'n platters make serving fun!

Whatcha Need: You'll need self-hardening caulk or tile grout, craft sticks or plastic knives, a white or pastel ceramic or heavy plastic plate for each person, varnish and brushes, and decorative trim items such as buttons, pebbles, small tiles, seashells, nuts and bolts, or beads.

Whatcha Do: Before class, collect an old dinner plate or platter for each person. White or pastel colors will work well, but avoid busy patterns, which will detract from the mosaic patterns kids will be adding to the rims of the plates. Heavy-gauge plastic plates and platters will also work. Using craft sticks or plastic knives, spread the rims of the plates with self-hardening caulk or tile grout, making sure the filler is a uniform ¼-inch thick around the rim. Gently press items such as buttons, pretty pebbles, or other materials into the caulk around the edge of the plate. Place the items close together, and continue in mosaic-style until the rims of the plates or platters are decorated. (Try to be sure all items are about the same height around the rim.) After the rims are decorated, set the plates in a sunny place to dry for a few hours. Then brush the edges of the plates with varnish to seal the caulk or grout. Tell kids they can use their perky platters to serve others at dinner and that the platters can be hand washed in sudsy water (no dishwashers).

BOTTLE GARDENS

Plant and watch these clever gardens grow!

Whatcha Need: You'll need newspapers, potting soil (with fertilizer), cotton balls, plastic spoons, long sticks or drinking straws, colored aquarium gravel, masking tape, a spray bottle filled with water, and a clear glass or plastic wide-mouth bottle for each person. (Be sure the bottles have lids or tops.) You'll also need a variety of small plants for kids to plant in their gardens. Most nurseries will provide small plants for a small cost. Of course, you can always plant flower seeds instead!

Whatcha Do: Choose medium to large-sized bottles with wide mouths for easy planting and watering. Plastic bottles or jugs are available at most craft stores, or use large mayonnaise-type bottles. Spread newspaper on a table, then show kids how to make the following planting tools:
  • *a trowel* (tape a long stick to the handle of a plastic spoon)
  • *a soil stomper* (tape a cotton ball to a long stick)
  • *a cleaning tool* (tape a second cotton ball to another long stick)
For each garden, place a 1-inch layer of colored aquarium gravel in the bottom of the bottle to help your garden drain. Then gently scoop potting soil over the gravel until the soil is at least 4 inches deep. Use the soil stomper to gently tamp down the potting soil. Show kids how to plant small potted plants in their garden (one or two small plants should do). If you're using seeds, demonstrate how to plant the seeds. Finally, use the cleaning tool to brush off any excess soil from the insides of the bottle, then spray the garden with water to dampen it well. Place the lid and set your bottle garden in a sunny location. Remind kids to gently water their gardens every other day and to replace the lids, which help the gardens retain moisture.

3 WHATTA FACE!

Fanciful faces that double as memo magnets.

Whatcha Need: You'll need black fine-tipped permanent markers, colored markers, tacky craft glue, scissors, white copy paper, and self-adhesive magnetic dots or tape. You'll also need at least three clear, flat decorative stones for each person (available in the plant department at craft stores).

Whatcha Do: On white copy paper, trace around the bottoms of the clear, flat stones. Have each child make at least three tracings. Use fine-tipped black permanent markers to draw eyes, noses, and mouths, then color the faces in whimsical ways. When the faces are finished, have kids cut them out. Glue each paper face to the flat bottom of a glass stone, then attach small self-adhesive magnetic dots or small squares of magnetic tape to the stones. (Trim any excess magnetic tape from around the bottoms of the stones.) Let kids play with their funny faces on metal filing cabinets, a refrigerator, or metal window frames. You may wish to invite kids to retell a variety of Bible stories using the faces as characters!

Whatcha Know!

For even easier faces, use yellow, green, red, and blue sticker dots—the kind you use for filing folders—instead of white copy paper. Or use cut-outs from the colorful comics found in weekend newspapers for another idea kids will love!

4 FOIL FRAMES

Frames as fun to make as they are useful!

Whatcha Need: You'll need thick cardboard, scissors, aluminum foil, tacky craft glue, rulers, and ballpoint pens. (If you really want a "wow 'em," have film and an instant camera ready to take cool pictures of your kids, then frame the pictures with the kids' creations.

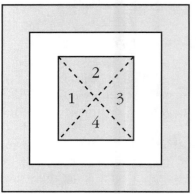

Whatcha Do: Older kids may like to cut their own frames from cardboard, but if your kids are a bit younger, cut out the frames before class as follows. Cut a 7-inch square of aluminum foil for each person. Cut a 6-inch cardboard square, then cut the center from the square, leaving a 1-inch border around the frame. Have kids spread glue on one side of the frame, then gently press the glued sides of the frames onto foil squares so the foil extends out an inch on all sides. Very gently cut an X through the foil in the hollow center of the frame (as in the diagram), and fold back triangles 1 through 4 and fold and glue them to the backs of the frames. On the fronts of the frames, use ballpoint pens to gently draw designs into the foil. Caution kids not to press too hard or the foil may tear. The foil will look similar to pressed metal designs. Finally, tape a picture or photograph to the back of the frame so it shows through the center opening. Use photos of the kids if you've taken them or let kids draw their own special pictures on 5½-inch squares of paper.

Whatcha Know!

Colored ink pens give a different look to the frames. Pink and green are especially nice on the shiny silver foil!

FUN FAMILY

Perky puppets that double as measuring spoons!

Whatcha Need: You'll need fine-tipped permanent markers, colored opaque paint markers (available at craft stores), thin sheets of craft foam (yellow, brown, red, and black), tacky craft glue, and a set of metal or plastic measuring spoons for each person.

Whatcha Do: Color the rounded backs of the spoons with flesh-tone paints (or fanciful colors if you're whimsical). Have kids paint one spoon for each member of their families. (If there are extra

spoons, use them to paint the faces of pets or close family friends!) When the paint is dried (several minutes), use fine-tipped permanent markers to add facial features (see samples in the margin). Cut very thin strips of craft foam for hair and use tacky craft glue to glue them in place on the tops of the spoons. Finally, use paint markers to add scarves, ties, buttons, aprons, collars, or other tidbits to the puppet people. As the puppet people dry, encourage kids to tell about why their families are important and how they work and play together. Have kids name ways God brings family members and families closer together and how they can thank God in their families for his love.

RAG-A-BALLS

Cute 'n colorful balls that are simple to make!

Whatcha Need: You'll need sheets of thin craft foam (one sheet for every two kids; available in craft departments and stores) in a variety of colors, scissors, and a plastic whiffle-type golf ball for each child (the kind with holes all over them).

Whatcha Do: Cut the sheets of craft foam into 3-by-1-inch strips. Show kids how to poke strips of foam into the holes on the whiffle golf balls, one strip per hole. Gently pinch the end of a foam strip and insert it halfway into a hole on a golf ball. When released, the foam will spread out and stay in the hole with a portion sticking out as in a rag ball. (If a foam strip falls out, simply replace it.) Let kids work to fill each hole on their golf balls. When finished, these colorful and lightweight balls are great for tossing and throwing indoors or out—and are safe and "ouchless"!

RINGS-N-THINGS

Two to wear and one to share—these rings are cool!

Whatcha Need: You'll need a variety of colors and sizes of chenille wire, scissors, and a selection of decorative shank buttons (the kind with plastic loops at the back).

Whatcha Do: Collect and purchase a wide variety of shank buttons from fabric shops, second-hand stores, and flea markets. These buttons come in a huge variety of colors and styles, including metallic, sparkly, bejeweled, and animal shapes. Be on the lookout for all types that both boys and girls would like. Plan on having three buttons for each child (plus extras to choose from) and three chenille wires for each person as well. Cut the chenille wires into 4-inch lengths.

To make these simple, yet simply elegant and fashionable rings, thread a chenille wire through the shank on the back of a button. Wrap the wire around your finger to size it, then twist the ends of the wire into a ring shape. Snip off any extra wire so it doesn't scratch your finger. As you work, remind kids that God's love for us is never-ending—just as a ring or circle never ends. Let kids make two rings to wear as reminders of God's unending love and one to share with a friend or family member as a friendship ring.

> ### Whatcha Know!
>
> Use more chenille wires and buttons to fashion bracelets, ankle bracelets, or cool necklaces to wear. These rings-n-things also make neat zipper pulls and shoelace decorations!

SUNNY SHINE-THROUGHS

Pleasin' plates that are perfect for sunny days!

Whatcha Need: You'll need tempera paints, plastic spoons, newspapers, colored vinyl or electrical tape, a hole punch, yarn or satin cord, and two clear plastic dinner plates for each child (available at most party stores).

Whatcha Do: Spread newspaper on a table and set out cups or muffin tins containing various colors of tempera paint, including red, yellow, pink, and blue. Have kids place drizzles and dribbles and small splotches of colorful paint in the centers of one of their plates. Then show kids how to gently "nest" another clear plate over the first to trap the paint between the plates and then squish it together. Help kids use colorful tape to seal the edges of their plates together. Then punch a hole through both plates along one edge and attach a yarn or cord loop for hanging. Place these unusual sun catchers in bright windows for striking effects!

NESTS-N-NIBBLERS

Birdfeeders serve God's creatures in a tasty way.

Whatcha Need: You'll need paint stir sticks (free from most paint stores), peanut butter, birdseed and unsalted sunflower seeds, plastic knives, paper grocery sacks, twine, scissors, and crepe paper.

Whatcha Do: Be sure you have a paint stir stick for each child. Have kids spread peanut butter on both sides of the paint sticks, leaving about 1 inch bare on each end of the sticks. Pour birdseed and unsalted sunflower seeds in a paper grocery sack, then drop in a buttery paint stick. Shake the paint stick until it's covered with birdseed. Tie a 3-foot length of twine to both ends of each stick. Cut varying lengths of crepe paper (4 to 8 inches). Tie or tape the crepe-paper strips up and down the length of the twine. (Birds and squirrels will love the bright paper and put it to use in building their nests!) Hang the nests-n-nibblers from branches or fence posts for birds and squirrels to enjoy!

For more feathery-friends projects, try these awesome ideas!

• Use plastic needlepoint canvas and thread nesting materials such as the following through the holes: paper, tissues, fiberfill, fabric scraps, craft feathers, long weeds and grasses, bits of foil, and yarn.

• Spread peanut butter over pine cones, then shake them in birdseed and hang from tree branches.

• Weave yarn and bits of paper loosely in the holes of a plastic berry basket. Tie a 2-foot string to opposite edges of the basket to hang in a tree. Finally, line the basket with foil and fill it with birdseed.

STORY MAGNETS
Fun puzzlers to help retell favorite Bible stories.

Whatcha Need: You'll need Bible-story scenes or pages from a coloring book (at least 7-by-6-inches), markers and crayons, scissors, and 3½-by-2-inch self-stick magnets (the kind made for attaching business cards, available in bulk at office supply stores). You'll need six magnets for each person.

> ## Whatcha Know!
>
> Older kids may wish to cut their larger puzzle pieces into smaller ones after the pictures are attached to the magnets. Use decorated envelopes to keep the puzzle pieces together.

Whatcha Do: Encourage kids to think about their favorite Bible stories and what makes them so special. Then invite kids to choose a page or scene from a coloring book to color using markers and crayons (or with colored pencils or water-color paints). After the scene is finished, flip the paper over and trace a block of 6 rectangles (two rows of three rectangles) using the self-stick magnets as patterns. Then cut out rectangles and stick them to the sticky sides of the magnets. When assembled, these mini puzzles will help kids retell Bible stories or special events from stories. Invite kids to get with partners to retell their stories by sticking their magnetic puzzle pieces to file cabinets, window frames, trash cans, or other metal objects. If there's time, you may want to visit a classroom of younger children and present your special magnetic stories to them!

SUPER CD CENTERS
Cool CDs that make awesome message centers!

Whatcha Need: You'll need paint pens, large paper clips, string, scissors, self-adhesive magnetic tape, small sticky note pads, glitter glue, and a discarded CD and small pencil for each person.

Whatcha Do: Collect the CDs and small pencils for each person. (Small pencils from a golf course work great!) Cut a 10-inch length of string for each person and have kids tie one end of their strings to large paper clips. Tie the other ends of the strings to the ends of the small pencils, then set them aside. Cut a 3-inch length of magnetic tape for each locker mate and stick the magnets to the sides of the CDs that have writing (not the shiny sides). Use paint pens and glitter glue to decorate the shiny sides of the CDs. While the paint dries, peel off clumps of fifteen to twenty note papers from the self-adhesive note pads to make smaller sticky note pads. Distribute a mini note pad to each person. When the paint dries, stick the note pads to the CDs, then poke the large paper clips, front to back, through the center holes on the CDs so the pencils are suspended on strings. Now kids are ready to jot down messages, telephone numbers, or other important info right at their lockers!

Try these other creative variations for kids' locker mates!

• Cut 3-inch circles from self-adhesive cork and make mini bulletin boards for lockers. You can use push pins to keep notes in place.

• Use tacky craft glue to attach small mirrors to the CDs.

• Write favorite Scripture verses around the outside edges of the CDs. Add as many verses, round and round, as will wind their way toward the center holes!

 # PERFECT POCKETS
Nifty pockets to hold all your treasures!

Whatcha Need: You'll need fine-tipped permanent black markers, clear plastic pencil cases (zippered type, one per child), white copy paper, scissors, tape, pencils, glass paints in a variety of colors, fine-tipped paintbrushes, water, newspapers, and paper towels.

Whatcha Do: Cover a table with newspapers. Cut sheets of white copy paper in half, then trim them so they fit inside of the clear pencil pockets (but don't place them inside the pockets yet). Invite kids to make practice designs on the papers using pencils. Geometric shapes, space designs, underwater scenes, and clouds and butterflies work well for designs.

When the designs are ready, tape them to the insides of the clear pockets. Then have kids begin by using fine-tipped permanent black markers to outline their designs on the outsides of the pockets. Fill in the shapes by painting them with colorful glass paints. (Use paper towels to wipe up any spills.) The paints will take an hour or so to dry, so be careful not to smudge the pockets. While the pockets are drying, visit about what kinds of treasures God gives us. Have kids take another piece of paper and list the many treasures God gives them. Have kids fold up their papers and place them in the Perfect Pockets as happy reminders of God's blessings. Tell kids they can keep special treasures in their pockets, such as neat pebbles, seashells, coins, pencils, or other goodies.

 # LIP SAVERS
Simple-to-make lip balm that is lip-smackin' good!

Whatcha Need: You'll need petroleum jelly, plastic spoons, small paper cups, concentrated flavorings such as cherry or raspberry, and plastic "bubbles" (the kind toys come in from vending machines) or other small containers.

Whatcha Do: Hand each child a plastic spoon and a small paper cup. Spoon one spoonful of petroleum jelly into each paper cup. Let kids add three drops of the flavorings they desire, then gently swirl the flavorings through the petroleum jelly. Spoon the soft lip gel into plastic bubbles or other small containers.

If you would rather make a more full-bodied lip balm, purchase beeswax at a health or craft store. Melt the beeswax in a microwave, heating the wax on high for 40 seconds, then in 10-second increments until the wax is melted. Add flavoring, then spoon the melted wax into containers. Refrigerate for twenty minutes or until the wax has solidified. For a fun twist, add two drops of food coloring to the wax.

NICE CUBE

A cool photo cube made from computer recyclables.

Whatcha Need: You'll need square floppy diskettes (five per child), tacky craft glue or a hot glue gun, plastic jewels, and family photos or markers and paper for kids to draw their families.

Whatcha Do: Collect old computer disks—the square diskettes that ran on older machines. You can find these diskettes in your attic or at thrift shops or can purchase them inexpensively from discount

stores. For each photo cube, glue the edges of four diskettes to one another to form a box, then glue the fifth diskette on the top (or bottom). Hot glue will make the gluing easier, but be sure to keep the glue gun out of reach of younger children. When the cube has been formed, let kids glue plastic jewels around the edges of the diskettes. Tape or glue a family photo (or photos, if you have more than one) on the sides of the cubes. If you don't have photographs, let kids cut paper to fit the sides of the cubes, then use markers to draw pictures of their families. These cool cubes can be turned upside down to be used as neat pencil holders. Simply glue the pictures on so they can be seen right-side up while pencils and pens are stored on a desk. What a super gift for dads or grandpas!

STONE WEAR

Older kids love these fun-to-make and wear stones.

Whatcha Need: You'll need jewelry wire (from craft stores), scissors, old socks or flannel scraps for polishing stones, satin or leather cord, crayons, aluminum foil, and access to an oven or toaster oven. You'll also need a variety of smooth, 2-to-3-inch stones. Plan on having at least two stones per person.

Whatcha Do: Cut the satin or leather cord into 16-inch lengths. (Boys will probably prefer leather over satin.) Cut 16-inch lengths of jewelry wire (it's thin, pliable wire and is easily snipped with scissors). Let kids use crayons to decorate the smooth stones of their choice. Thick bands across the rocks or thick swirls work best. When the stones are colored, place them on foil and pop them in a 350-degree oven for about three minutes or until the crayon wax is melted. Cool the stones, then have kids use soft cloths to polish the stones. Show kids how to wrap wire around their stones. Wind the wire once around the stones lengthwise, and once around widthwise before twisting the wire ends together in a small loop at the tops of the stones. Thread cord through the small loops to suspend the stones as pendants on necklaces. If there's enough time and materials, kids can also make ankle and wrist bracelets or zipper pulls for backpacks. Or try making pebble pendants— instead of threading cord through the loop, slide the loop onto a safety pin to wear! String several stones of various sizes on a large safety or diaper pin, add a few beads, and this stone wear becomes an awesome Mom's Day or Valentine's Day gift!

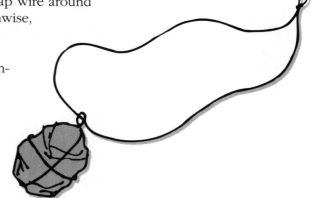

16. WALK ON!

Walking sticks remind kids to be good leaders.

Whatcha Need: You'll need thick 3-foot sticks or 1-inch-by-3-foot dowel rods, colored vinyl tape, feathers, dried grasses, leaves, yarn or ribbon, and brightly colored paint pens.

Whatcha Do: Have kids choose their walking sticks. Embellish the sticks by wrapping colored tape up and down the sticks or in stripes around the tops and bottoms. Tape on feathers, leaves, or dried grasses. Use paint pens to decorate the wood. Finally, tie on various lengths of yarn or ribbon at the tops of the sticks. As kids work, remind them how Moses used a walking stick to help as he led the people in following God. Ask kids to tell why being a good leader for others is related to being a follower of God's. After the sticks are finished and have dried, take turns playing Follow the Leader inside or outdoors.

> ### Whatcha Know!
>
> Have kids write Scripture verses about following God or being good leaders on small cards. Punch holes in the corners and tie the cards to the walking sticks. As you walk along, try learning the verses by heart!

17 ROSY POSIES

Cute pins that are perfect for moms or sisters!

Whatcha Need: You'll need tiny silk flower bouquets (available at craft stores), green florist's tape, craft sticks, 1½-inch-long pin backs (from craft stores), glitter glue, and tacky craft glue or a hot glue gun. (Use a large pair of scissors or a small coping saw to cut the craft sticks into 1-inch lengths.)

Whatcha Do: If you cannot find small bouquets, kids can make their own from small silk flowers and leaves. Arrange the florals into 3-inch-tall bouquets and secure the stems using florist's tape. Have kids take their small flower bouquets and place a section of craft stick against the backs of the stems. Let kids work in pairs as they wrap a 4-inch section of florist's tape around the stems and craft stick. After the craft stick and stems have been wrapped, use tacky glue or a hot glue gun to glue a pin back to the flat side of the wrapped craft stick. (A hot glue gun will work best, but be sure to keep it out of the reach of younger children.) Finally, add a bit of sparkle by tipping the flowers and leaves with a bit of glitter glue. Set the pins aside to dry, then wrap them in tissue paper for adorable gifts!

ZIPPY WRIST WRAPS

Kids love these awesome wrist wraps—make several!

Whatcha Need: You'll need paint pens, scissors, tacky craft glue, self-adhesive hoop-and-loop fasteners, plastic or metallic jewels or buttons (in fun shapes such as stars or diamonds), and a 6- or 7-inch zipper for each person.

Whatcha Do: Cut the self-adhesive hook-and-loop fasteners into small rectangles (½-by-¾-inch), two sets of fasteners for each person. Kids may wish to work with partners, since an extra pair of hands is

a big help! Wrap a zipper around your wrist so you like the fit, then notice where the zipper ends overlap. Peel the backing from the hook-and-loop fasteners and stick them to the ends of the zipper where they overlapped. (Remind kids how to attach hook-and-loop fasteners so they work!) Set the wrist wraps face up on a table. On the fabric portion of the zippers, add designs using paint pens and plastic jewels. Remind kids that simple designs often work the best! Allow the paints to dry for several minutes before wrapping and attaching the way-cool wraps around your wrists.

POUND-A-ROUNDS
Unusual wall hangings that are sooo fun to make!

Whatcha Need: You'll need 8-inch squares of white cotton fabric, 6-inch round plastic quilting hoops, string or satin cord, hammers, newspapers, scissors, and a variety of fresh flowers and leaves (from your garden or scraps from a florist shop).

Whatcha Know!

Use rectangle-shaped fabric and hammer out your designs. Fray the edges of the fabric, iron gently, and place inside a decorated shirt-sized gift box to use as a tray and liner for rolls or desserts at the dinner table.

Whatcha Do: Kids may enjoy going on a walk to find their own flowers and leaves to use for this project. Dandelions, buttercups, lilacs, geraniums, petunias, or other fresh flowers and flowering weeds work well. Try to find a variety of colors, including yellow, red, purple, green, and even orange or pink. After the flowers and leaves are collected, spread newspapers on the ground on a solid wood or cement floor or sidewalk. Place the white fabric squares on the newspapers. Show kids how to arrange their flowers and leaves on one half of their cotton squares, then fold over the other half. Using a hammer, gently pound the flowers and leaves several times to release their natural dyes and scents. Then carefully open the fabric and marvel at the pretty designs! After the designs are complete, attach the plastic quilting hoops over the designs and trim off excess fabric from the back. Tie on string or satin cord loops so the Pound-a-Rounds can be hung on walls or in windows.

CARD CUDDLERS
Cute cuddlers to hold special reminders!

Whatcha Need: You'll need colorful clay (self-hardening or Fimo-type clay), plastic knives, scissors, colored paper, and markers.

Whatcha Do: Make one of these nifty Card Cuddlers before class to show kids how they work. Begin by cutting colored paper into 2-by-3-inch note cards. Cut at least ten cards for each person. Mold colorful clay into a rectangular base that measures about 4-inches long, ½-inch deep, and 2-inches wide. Using a plastic knife, dig out a ¼-inch-deep trough in the base closer to one edge than the opposite edge. (See the illustration on page 18.) Make the trough almost go from one end of the base to the other and about ½-inch wide. This is the trough in which the small note cards will sit upright. Next, form a colorful clay flower or animal such as a kitty, lion, duck, or frog and set it on the wider back edge of the base. (Be sure the animal fits on the edge without blocking the trough.) Use the plastic knife to blend the bottom edges of the clay flower or animal into the edge of the base so it stays in place. Let the clay harden according to the directions on the package. (If the flower or animal pops off after drying, simply use tacky craft glue to attach it again!) As the clay dries, have kids write reminders of how they can worship God on the small note cards. Suggestions might include: "Pray today," "Give thanks to God," "Keep a happy heart," and "Forgive others even when it's hard." You may wish to include favorite Scripture verses in your selection of reminders. After the Card Cuddlers are dry, place the reminder cards in the trough to read each day.

LIGHT UP THE WORLD
Fun-to-make candles that light up kids' smiles!

Whatcha Need: You'll need a baby-food jar and lid for each person, wax paraffin (available at grocery and craft stores), large paper clips, food coloring, plastic drinking straws (two per child), candle wicking (from craft stores), scissors, colorful candy sprinkles or glitter dust, and scented oils (if you wish). You'll also need access to a microwave oven or an old electric skillet to melt the paraffin in. (You may choose to use pre-made candle-wax chips available at most craft stores instead of paraffin wax.)

Whatcha Do: Cut the candle wicking into 3½-inch lengths. Have kids tie one end of the wicking around the center of a drinking straw and the other end around a large paper clip. Set aside the wicks for now. Melt the wax paraffin according to the package directions. (If you're using an electric skillet, simply heat the wax on medium to low heat until it's melted.) Carefully pour the melted paraffin into baby-food jars. Let kids use plastic drinking straws to stir in food coloring, then swirl candy sprinkles or glitter dust through the wax. (If you want, add scented oils at this time.) Use the stirring straw to gently poke the paper clips down through the center of the wax, then rest the drinking straw with the wick attached across the center of the jar rim. (Tape the straws in place if needed.) Allow the wax to cool completely. Remind kids to have an adult light the candle at your dinner table. For a different look, drop in shaved bits of crayons instead of glitter or candies.

MESSAGE CENTER
Get organized with this awesome message center!

Whatcha Need: You'll need white self-adhesive paper, self-stick magnetic strip, scissors, a roll of self-adhesive cork, permanent markers, push pins, dry erase markers (one per child), string, rulers, brushed flannel fabric, and an old cookie sheet for each person (the kind with a small hole in one end of the edge).

Whatcha Do: Check garage sales, thrift stores, and second-hand shops for old cookie sheets. Most have a small hole at one or both ends of the rim, but if you cannot find this type, others will still work. Cut string into 12-inch lengths and the flannel fabric into 5-inch squares, one per child. Have kids cover one half of their cookie sheets with white self-adhesive paper and the other half with self-adhesive cork. On the white sides of the cookie sheets, use rulers to mark off a week-long calendar grid, as shown in the

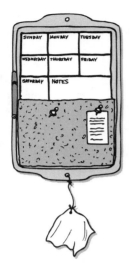

illustration. Use permanent markers to make the grids and add the names of the days of the week. Under the week-long calendar, use a permanent marker to write the word "notes." (The space here can be used for kids to write special notes or messages during the week.) If you're using cookie sheets with holes, tie one end of each string to a flannel square and the other end of the string through the hole on the cookie sheet. These cloths are the erasers. (If your cookie sheets don't have holes, attach 1-inch lengths of self-stick magnetic tape to the cloth erasers and stick them to the edges of the cookie sheets.) Cut small pieces of magnetic tape and stick them to the dry-erase markers. Give each child one marker to stick to the edge of his message center. Finally, place two push pins in the cork side of each center. Kids can set their message centers on desks or tables to help keep track of their busy days.

KEY STONES

Nifty rocks to hold extra keys or secret messages!

Whatcha Need: You'll need small plastic or cardboard boxes (with an end that opens or removable tops), aluminum foil, brown shoe polish, soft rags, and a can of self-hardening foam insulation sealant (available at hardware stores or home centers).

Whatcha Do: Since the insulation foam you'll be using takes a couple of hours to harden, you may wish to make this a two-part project—but it's definitely worth the wait! Find small, wide boxes made from plastic or cardboard. The boxes will need to have one end that opens so that keys, messages, and other important treasures can be placed inside the finished stone. You'll need one box for each person. Place foil on a table and set the boxes on the foil with the sides that open facing downward on the foil. Shake the foam sealant, then let kids spray the foam (like shaving cream) over the three sides of their boxes. After the "stones" have hardened, rub shoe polish over them to give them more of a "stone" finish. Use old rags to wipe of excess polish. Place keys or other secret stuff in the stone and place it open side down in a garden, on a desk, or anyplace you want to camouflage it!

> ### Whatcha Know!
>
> The stones can be painted with stone-type spray paint available at hardware or discount stores, and if the boxes are plastic, they'll be weather-proof, too!

HANGING GARDENS

Unusual balls are really hanging gardens.

Whatcha Need: You'll need sphagnum moss (available at craft stores and nurseries), a dishpan with water, newspapers, paper towels, a ball of twine, scissors, sticks, and a variety of seeds such as beans, peas, marigolds, radishes, squash, and pumpkins.

Whatcha Do: Have kids take a handful of sphagnum moss and dip it in the dishpan of water. Wring out the excess water and mold the moss into a ball about the size of a grapefruit, adding more damp moss if needed. (If the moss balls are still drippy, blot them with paper towels.) Then have kids work in pairs to wind a 2-foot piece of twine around and around the moss ball. Tie off the twine. Cut another 18-inch length of twine and tie it to twine at the top of the ball for hanging. Use a stick to poke holes in the moss ball, then poke seeds down into the holes. Pinch the damp moss over the holes. Hang your newly planted gardens in a sunny window and dampen them with water each day be spraying them heavily with water. If the moss is kept moist, the hanging gardens should sprout within about seven to ten days. As the plants grow, they will tumble downward and look lovely!

For a variation on this craft, fill a self-sealing plastic freezer bag halfway with sphagnum moss, dampen with water, and "plant" your seeds in the moss. Poke air holes in the bag and keep the moss moist. Tape or tie a ribbon hanger to the top of the bag and suspend it in a window.

25 COOL COASTERS
Fun coasters to use with your friends and family.

Whatcha Need: You'll need sheets of thin craft foam in a variety of colors, tacky craft glue, scissors, glitter glue, pencils, paint pens, and permanent markers. (If you choose white craft foam instead of colored, permanent markers will work instead of paint pens.)

Whatcha Do: Have kids work in pairs to trace their hands and footprints (with socks on) on thin craft foam. You may wish to have each child do one print of his hand and one of his foot. Carefully cut out the foam prints. Invite kids to use paint pens, glitter glue, and permanent markers to embellish their prints in any way they choose. Girls may wish to make colored fingernails or toenails; boys may enjoy drawing cool tennis shoes or gloves on their prints. Add rings 'n things with glitter glue. Kids can personalize their prints by adding their names or writing special messages across the shapes. Briefly discuss how God protects us, then explain how the coasters can be used at home to put hot or cold drinks on to protect the furniture.

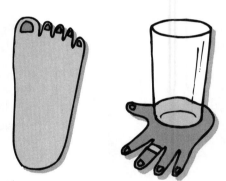

For another cool coaster idea, stick 3-inch circles of self-adhesive cork to the shiny sides of discarded CDs or floppy diskettes. Decorate the edges of the coasters with paint pens or plastic jewels. How about embellishing a mug to go with the coasters and giving them as great gifts to someone special?

MORE GREAT GAMES

Rowdy races, daring dodge ball, nifty relays, and more team up for rib-tickling fun— and loads of communication and cooperation!

A Bit of Background

Hopscotch, tag, tug-of-war, charades, four-square—what was your favorite game as a child? Games come in such a variety of shapes and sizes, it may be hard to choose! From indoor to outdoor, cooperative to gently competitive, small-group to individual relays and races, games are perennial favorites with kids of all ages. But games aren't just for fun—they're for learning, too! Adding quality games to your children's programming offers kids the chance to

- increase communication skills,
- explore what cooperation means,
- build community and teamwork skills,
- nurture friendships,
- tame the wiggles, and
- learn about good sportsmanship.

Great games can help kids feel part of a team, part of a larger group—just like their teamwork in Christ's body of believers! And many games can emphasize Christian values such as cooperation, kindness, sharing, obeying rules, and being helpful.

Many teachers feel that cooperative games—games with no winners or losers—are the only kind of games for their children. But gentle competition need not be ignored. Achieving the highest number of points isn't the only way to score a game. Look for innovative scoring that encourages kids instead of discouraging them, such as awarding points for endurance, style, imagination, kindness, or other positive qualities. Older kids especially enjoy a bit of healthy competition and striving to be the best they can be.

Become familiar with the games in the Great Games section of *More 200+ Activities for Children's Ministry* and you'll be ready at a wiggle's notice for fun and frolic kids will love! Here are a few helpful hints to get you started.

* **Use crepe-paper streamers for goal lines, starting lines, and game boundaries. Tape them in place or use rocks to hold them on outdoor fields.**

* **Make bright number and color cubes to roll for turns in a game, number of moves, or other ideas. Simply cover six-sided boxes (any size) with construction paper or colored self-adhesive paper. Use permanent markers to add numerals or color words. Kids love rolling these game cubes!**

* **Ways to "award" winning teams might include being first in line for water, choosing the next game to play, giving high fives to each other, or even getting back scratches from the other team!**

TIGER TAILS

Try to capture each other's tiger tails.

Whatcha Need: You'll need four 3-foot lengths of cloth or rope. (If your class is very large, plan on a rope or cloth strip for every four kids.)

Whatcha Do: Form four teams and have team members stand in a line holding the waists of the players in front of them. These will be the "tigers." Hand the last person in each tiger formation a long cloth or rope "tail." Have kids tuck the tiger tails into their belts or waistbands so they drag on the ground. Explain that in this game, tigers must run as a team and try to step on each other's tails. If a tiger captures another tiger's tail, the tiger without the tail must sit in place and the other tiger adds that tail to make two tails, and so on. The last tiger still prowling wins. Play several rounds and switch tiger teams often to give kids a chance to play with different team members. End with tiger teams giving each other big high fives.

SHIP IN A BOTTLE

A game of skill for a cold or rainy day.

Whatcha Need: You'll need string or twine, scissors, a wide-mouth jar or tall plastic drinking glass for every four kids, and a hinge-style clothespin for each child.

Whatcha Do: Before class, cut a 3½-foot length of string or twine for each person. Hand kids the string and have them tie the strings around their waists. Clip a clothespin "ship" on the end of each string. Form teams of four and have kids number off by fours. Then hand each team a bottle or plastic drinking glass. Explain that in this game, you'll call out a number between one and four. Kids with the corresponding numbers must stand over the containers and try to lower their ships into the bottles. When a ship is completely inside a bottle, the team shouts, "Ship ahoy!" Score two points to the first team to shout, and score one point each to the other teams. Continue calling different numbers until everyone has had at least one turn. End by having each entire team try to lower all of their ships into their bottles at once.

Try these variations for even more fun. Tie the strings to your elbows, feet, knees, or ears instead of your waists. Set the bottles at one end of the room and turn this game into a relay race. Try blindfolding the player with the ship and have the rest of the team guide the ship into the bottle by giving verbal directions.

COLOR-CALL BALL

This is an awesome outdoor game for any age!

Whatcha Need: You'll need a playground ball.

Whatcha Do: Choose one player to be the first caller and hand her the ball. Gather the rest of the players around the caller and assign them colors such as red, yellow, blue, green, orange, and purple. Tell kids to remember their colors. The caller will toss the ball high and kids will scatter. When the ball is caught again by the caller, she calls, "Color freeze!" and kids must stop in their tracks. The caller may take five giant steps toward another player. The caller has two guesses as to the color that player is. If she guesses correctly, she tries to tag that player by tossing the ball. If the player is tagged, the caller and player switch roles (and the caller assumes the player's color). In the event the player is not tagged, the caller must toss the ball again after gathering everyone together. Continue playing until most players have been the caller. End by having players give each other high fives for being good sports.

PICKLE JAR

A great game of cooperation and communication.

Whatcha Need: You'll need no extra materials. (Nice, isn't it?)

Whatcha Do: Have kids stand in a medium-sized circle. Explain that the circle is a pickle jar and that kids are the pickles and will soon be in a big pickle! Have everyone extend his right hand into the center of the circle and take hold of someone else's hand. Now repeat the process joining left hands. When everyone is holding hands of other pickles in the pickle jar, challenge kids to see if they can untangle the pickle they're in by ducking under people, carefully stepping over them, or turning around. Tell kids they cannot let go of the hands they're holding, so communication and cooperation of all pickles is a premium! Allow several minutes to solve the pickle. If kids are still quite tangled, allow everyone to drop their right hands and continue. Older kids may enjoy a livelier version of Pickle Jar: Hold someone else's hand in your right hand and hold another person's foot with your left hand. Whatta pickle!

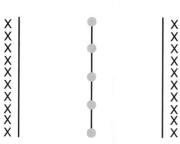

Whatcha Know!

Kids love sharing sweet and sour pickles after a rousing game of Pickle Jar. Visit about how communication and cooperation helped in the game and how it helps us serve God as well.

FIVE-PIN SOCCER

Score goals and switch teams—awesome fun!

Whatcha Need: You'll need five plastic soda bottles (and caps), a soccer ball or playground ball, and masking tape.

Whatcha Do: Set up the play areas as follows. Stick a 10-foot masking tape line down the center of your play area and two masking tape lines on either side of the center line and at least 12 feet apart. Fill the soda bottles a third full with sand, small gravel, rice, or water to give them some stability. Position the soda bottles every 2 feet across the center line. Form two teams and have players stand along the sidelines, each team facing the other team. Explain that in this soccer game, players try to kick field goals by knocking over soda bottles. If a player kicks over a bottle, she must run to set up the bottle, then join the opposite team. (Just think of all the people you'll get to play with!) Tell each player to remember the number of bottles he or she kicks over. (The points will be added up at the end of the game.) Play continues for five minutes, then call time. Add up the number of points scored by each person on the teams. Form two new teams with equal numbers of members to play again.

BUMBER SHOOTS

Young kids really go for this bouncy counting game!

Whatcha Need: You'll need an umbrella, masking tape, and four tennis balls.

Whatcha Do: Before playing, tape a masking-tape square to the floor, making each side 5 to 6 feet long. Set up the umbrella in an upside-down position in the center of the square. Form four groups and have each group stand along one side of the masking-tape square. Hand each group a tennis ball. Explain that in this game kids will try to bounce the tennis balls into the open umbrella on a certain number of counts, from one to four. For example, if the leader calls out "three," the players with the tennis balls try to make the balls bounce three times before landing in the umbrella. If a team can land its tennis ball on the right number of bounces, they score a point. (If the ball misses the umbrella or the number of bounces, no points are scored.) If the leader says, "Bumber shoots," any number of bounces is allowed and one point is scored just for landing the ball in the umbrella. Continue until one team scores five points, then switch teams.

BIG-FOOT RACERS

This silly relay is loads of foot-ticklin' fun!

Whatcha Need: You'll need scissors, duct tape, large cardboard boxes, six plastic cups, small balls (such as golf balls or Ping-Pong balls).

Whatcha Do: Place plastic cups in two rows of three and about 3 feet apart down the playing area. Have kids quickly make Big-Foot Racers to wear by cutting out 2-foot-long footprints from cardboard. (You may want a pair to use as patterns according to the outline in the margin.) After the pairs of big feet are cut out, have kids tape them to the bottoms of their shoes using duct tape. (Wrap the duct tape up and over kids' shoes and the bottoms of the cardboard feet.) Form two Big-Foot teams—the Sasquatch and the Yetis—and have teams stand in two lines about 15 feet from the first cups. Hand the first two players in each line a small ball. Explain that in this silly relay players must roll the ball using their feet and go in and out around the plastic cups on their side of the playing area. Then players roll the balls back to their lines and the next players go. Continue until one team has completed its turns, then give a loud "grunt" to signify the finish. Try this same over-sized idea by having kids cut out huge cardboard hands and taping them to their own hands. Then roll the balls around the cups or play a lively game of Sasquatch basketball!

SPOT TAG

Tag each other with stickers—then pass them on!

Whatcha Need: You'll need scissors and sheets of colorful sticker dots (from office supply stores). These sticker dots come in four-color packages with green, red, yellow, and blue stickers. You'll need three or four colors for this game (depending on your class size).

Whatcha Do: Cut the sticker dots into four-dot clumps and leave the stickers attached to the backing paper for now. Form three or four teams and designate the teams the colors that correspond to the sticker colors. Hand each player a clump of four spots of their corresponding colors. For example, a player on the red team will receive a clump of four red spots and so on. Explain that in this wild tag game players are to tag others with spots but not get caught at the end of the game wearing one of their own colored spots. Explain that spots can be peeled off and used again to tag other players; however, each person can only tag another player with one spot at a time. Once a player is tagged with a red spot, for example, that player cannot be tagged by another red spot until she has gotten rid of the spot by tagging another player. (She can be tagged by other colors of spots.) Tell kids they'll have three minutes to get rid of all their spots and not be caught with one of their own colors!

> ### Whatcha Know!
>
> Play the game again, but if a player is tagged with his color spot at any time during the game, he is out and sits down. Play continues until only one player is left standing.

FLYIN' GOLF

Kids fly high when they play this round of golf.

Whatcha Need: You'll need a bolt of brightly colored ribbon, paper plates, colorful permanent markers, four large construction-paper stars, scissors, and a margarine lid for each person.

Whatcha Do: This great golf game is perfect for outdoors, but it can also be played in a large indoor area such as a gymnasium, cafeteria, or large classroom. (Clear a large playing area if indoors.) Before playing, have kids help set up a golf course according to the illustration in the margin. Use lengths of ribbon to mark the "fairways" leading to each hole. Place a numbered paper plate at the end of each hole and a construction-paper star to mark the tee-off area. Adjust the length of each fairway according to if you're playing indoors or out. Indoor fairways can be as short as 6-feet long, but outdoor fairways can be 20-feet long. Let kids decorate their margarine-lid "flyers" with permanent markers. Then form four teams and have each team stand at a different star. Have players take turns tossing their flyers toward the corresponding paper-plate "hole." Count the number of tosses to reach the hole. Continue playing each hole on your course. When everyone has played all four holes, add up your team scores. The team with the lowest score chooses which hole to begin from in the next round. Change teams often so kids play with other groups.

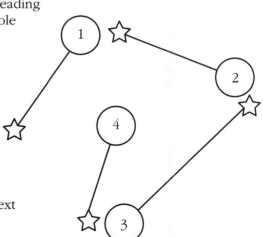

BEAT THE BUNNY

A simple race that's fun for all ages and abilities.

Whatcha Need: You'll need a small and a large item such as a crayon and chalkboard eraser.

Whatcha Do: Seat kids in a circle and hand one person the small item, which is the "bunny," and another child the large item, which is the "farmer." Explain that in this hand-to-hand race the farmer will chase the bunny around the circle. The object is for the bunny to return to its original starting place before being tagged by the farmer. Tell kids that the bunny gets a three-count head start before the farmer starts racing after him. Both bunny and farmer can change directions around the circle as needed, but if the bunny is tagged, the child holding the bunny has to hop to a different place to sit in the circle, then play begins again. (If the farmer doesn't catch the bunny, kids give each other high fives and begin a new race at new starting points.)

Try these tips and variations for different play.
- For young kids, allow the bunny to change directions, but not the farmer.
- Play this race like musical chairs: When the bunny is caught, the child holding it is out. When the farmer fails to catch the bunny, the child holding the farmer is out.

BUBBLE WALKING

A tactile race that gets lots of bubbly laughter!

Whatcha Need: You'll need scissors and a roll of large bubble wrap (available at office stores or packaging centers).

Whatcha Do: Cut two 5-foot lengths of large bubble wrap and lay them on the floor side by side and about 4 feet apart. Form two teams and have each team divide in half and stand at opposite ends of their length of bubble wrap. Explain that in this relay race players must walk softly across the bubble wrap, trying not to pop the bubbles. When the first players reach their partners on the other sides of the wrap, they tap their partners, then go to the back of the line to sit down. The partners then walk back across the bubble wrap to the other side and tap the next person in line, and so on. The first team to have all the players seated wins. Try other ways to cross the bubble wrap, such as crawling, rolling, "scooching," or tiptoeing backwards.

Team A 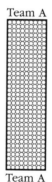 Team B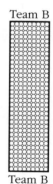

Team A   Team B

BLANKET VOLLEYBALL

A new twist on an old favorite!

Whatcha Need: You'll need thick yarn or rope, two old blankets or large bedsheets, and a volleyball or playground ball. (Power Hint: This game is best when played outdoors!)

Whatcha Do: Place a 10-foot length of thick yarn or rope across your playing area as a "net." Form two teams and have teams stand on opposite sides of the net. Have each team stand around the outside edges of an old blanket or bedsheet and hold the edges up. (Be sure there's a child positioned at each corner of the blanket or sheet.) Explain that this game is played much like regular volleyball, except the ball will be vaulted to one another by way of the blankets! Practice once by having one of the teams "serve" the volleyball by placing the ball in the middle of the blanket. Lower the blanket, then raise it quickly as a team to allow the ball to become airborne. The opposing team must catch the volleyball in their blanket and toss it back again. Play continues until the ball is not caught, then one point is scored for the team that volleyed the ball. Set a point limit for each game, such as ten points. For even more fun with a larger group, have three or four teams playing with two balls simultaneously.

MAGIC CARPET RIDE
Teamwork solves this fun puzzle in record time!

Whatcha Need: You'll need two large bedsheets, blankets, or plastic shower-curtain liners.

Whatcha Do: Form two teams and hand each team a bedsheet, blanket, or shower-curtain liner. Direct team members to stand on the sheets and tell kids these are their magic carpets and that you want to take a ride. However, there is one big problem: You're not going anywhere because your carpet is upside down and can't fly. Explain that the object of this game is to flip the carpets without anyone stepping off. Players may use hands, feet, and heads to solve this puzzling predicament. The team that reverses its carpet first without anyone stepping off is the winning team. Play again by switching around team members. Try solving the puzzling by sitting and flipping the carpets over. This is a great game for older kids and encourages loads of cooperation and communication!

ZIB-ZUB
A perfect indoor game for a dreary day!

Whatcha Need: You'll need markers, six index cards, a paper lunch sack, and enlarged photocopies on stiff paper of the monster patterns from this activity: Zib and Zub (page 107).

Whatcha Do: Copy on stiff paper the comical monsters Zib and Zub. Color the monsters with bright markers or crayons. (Laminate them for added durability if you desire.) Label six index cards as follows, one phrase per card: "Before Zib," "Zib," "After Zib," "Before Zub," "Zub," "After Zub." Place the index cards in the lunch sack and seat kids in a circle "washtub" on the floor. Hand one person the Zib cutout and another the Zub. Explain that in this passing game, everyone will repeat the following rhyme as the monsters are passed around the washtub circle:

Rub-a-dub, Zip and Zub—
Pass them around the washing tub!

When the rhyme stops on the word "tub," pull out an index card and read it aloud. If the card states, "before Zib (or Zub)," the player that is about to receive that character is out and becomes the next card reader. If the card says, "after Zib (or Zub)," the player that just had that character is out and becomes the next card reader. And if the card says a character's name, the player holding the character is out and is the next reader. (Refer to the following chart to become familiar with who becomes "out.")

Before Zib (or Zub) = the next player to get the character is out.
After Zib (or Zub) = the player who just had the character is out.
Zib (or Zub) = the player holding the character is out.

After reading the card and establishing who is out and the next reader, close the gap in the washtub circle and continue passing. Play until only one person is left. For extra excitement and fun, call out "switch" in the middle of passing to quickly reverse the passing direction. Other variations might be passing Zib and Zub in different ways, such as under the legs or behind backs.

WASH-DAY BLUES
Fast-paced tag that's great indoors or out!

Whatcha Need: You'll need masking tape and four hinge-style clothespins for each player.

Whatcha Do: Use masking tape to set up the boundaries of your play area indoors. (If you're playing outside, omit the tape.) Try an unusual shape such as a triangle with 10-foot sides or a hexagon with 6-foot sides. Hand each person four clothespins and explain that in this tag-like game players are to try to pin clothespins to four different articles of clothing: two shoes, pants (or skirt), and a sleeve. (Use collars or hems if there are sleeveless shirts.) Tell kids that the object of the game is to get rid of as many clothespins as they can and to receive as few as possible in the allotted time (usually two minutes). Point out that they can only clip one pin at a time to any one player but can return later to add another clothespin.

For an extra challenge, try these cool variations.
• Shoe Tag—Clothespins can only be placed on shoes and shoelaces.
• Steal the Pins—Clip pins to the hem of your shirt and try to snatch as many of someone else's pins as possible in the time allotted. Only one pin may be taken at one time.
• Melt-Away Tag—One person is the Tagger and one the Melter (who has all the clothespins). When someone is tagged, he freezes until the Melter clips a clothespin on him to thaw him out. Try to tag everyone in three minutes.

BOLA JUMPING
Play with partners, teams, or as solo jumpers.

Whatcha Need: You'll need two old socks, dried beans or rice (or sand), scissors, and 6-foot lengths of ribbon in the following colors: red, green, blue, and yellow.

Whatcha Do: Make a bola by tying a 3-foot length of red ribbon to 1-foot lengths of green, blue, and yellow ribbon to form one long ribbon. Make two of these ribbon rainbows. Then fill two socks with dried beans, rice, or sand and tie the socks to the ends opposite the red ribbons. (Cut off any extra sock around the ankle.) Hand the bolas to two kids, who will be the first twirlers. The rest of the kids will be jumpers. Have the twirlers begin twirling the bolas low to the ground around and around in a circle. (It may take a few tries to get the bolas moving in circles that don't bump into each other.) Kids are to jump over the bolas as they swing around. Twirlers may lift the bolas slightly off the ground or twirl at different speeds to try to get jumpers to miss. A miss occurs when the bola is stepped on or bumps someone's foot or leg. If a player is tagged by the bola, he must sit out until five players have been tagged and a new round begins. The first player out each round becomes the next twirler.

PARTY PRANKS
Get kids giggling in no time!

Whatcha Need: You'll need a paper party hat and balloon for each player.

Whatcha Do: Purchase inexpensive party hats or have kids make their own for this game. (Keep the hats and extra balloons in a sack or box so you can play this festive game again in a snap!) Choose one player to be the party host (or hostess), and have that person stand at one end of the room holding a balloon. Have the rest of the kids don their party hats and blow up their balloons and tie them off. Position kids at the end of the room opposite the party host. The party host will toss his balloon in the air while all the party goers walk slowly forward laughing and bopping their balloons up and down. When the party host's balloon touches the floor, party goers must freeze in place holding their balloons and not laughing, giggling, or smiling. If the party host spies someone still giggling or smiling or a balloon on the floor, that party goer must return to the starting place and begin again. Play continues until one player has tagged the party host. This player becomes the next party host and hands her hat to the former host, who will now be a party goer.

BIBLE BOOKS
A fun game to teach where Bible books are found.

Whatcha Need: You'll need markers, poster board, two Ping-Pong balls, self-adhesive hook-and-loop fastener tape, scissors, masking tape, and 3 yards of solid-colored flannel, felt, or brushed cotton fabric.

Whatcha Do: Tape or otherwise fasten the large flannel piece to a wall, bulletin board, or door. Stick a length of tape down the center of the flannel. Place a masking-tape line about 5 feet in front of the flannel as a throw line. Cut poster board into two 6-by-10-inch rectangles. Write "Old Testament" on one rectangle and "New Testament" on the other. Tape each sign to one side of the flannel. Stick small pieces of self-adhesive hook-and-loop fastener tape (the rough portions) to the Ping-Pong balls so that when they are thrown against the flannel they will stick to it. Form two teams and position them at the throw line in two rows. Hand the first players in each line a ball. Explain that you will name a book of the Bible, then players can throw their balls to either the New or Old Testament side to indicate where the book is found in the Bible. If correct, score one point for the team. Play continues either until everyone has had a turn or one teams scores fifteen points.

For extra fun, try these variations:
- Name characters from either the Old or New Testaments and toss balls to the correct sides.
- Make True and False or Yes and No cards, then attach them to the flannel. Ask questions about Bible stories, people, or events and have kids throw the balls to the correct side.

GUARD YOUR FAITH

Classic dodge ball with a new attitude!

Whatcha Need: You'll need a playground ball, plastic cups, scissors, string, and balloons.

Whatcha Do: Have kids get in pairs or trios and hand each person an 18-inch length of string and a balloon. Blow up and tie off the balloons and tie the strings around the knots on the balloon. Have kids then tie the strings to one of their feet at the ankle. Hand each pair or trio a plastic cup and have kids spread out around the playing area, placing their cups upside down on the floor. Explain that in this game of guarding kids not only have to guard their cups from being knocked over by the ball but must also not pop their balloons by stepping on them as they play! Players may roll the ball toward someone's cup to

try and knock it over. If a cup is knocked over, those partners must set their cups aside and play by holding arms around each other's shoulders for balance and may only hop on the feet with the balloons attached. If a balloon pops, that player is out of the game. Play continues for ten minutes or until there is only one cup left standing.

BOM-BOM
This game of charades is full of lively laughter.

Whatcha Need: You'll need no extra game props.

Whatcha Do: Form two teams, team A and team B, and have each team choose a spokesperson. Position the teams at opposite ends of the playing area. (Make sure there is at least 15 feet of space between the two teams.) Explain that in this game teams take turns acting out categories of things such as types of cars or kinds of furniture, then must run across the playing area without being tagged by opposing team members. Team A will be the first to act out a category, which you will whisper to them. The team then huddles to decide how to act out the category. After a few moments, team A walks slowly toward team B. Teams chant the following words:

Team A: ***Bom, Bom, Bom—here we come.***
Team B: ***Are you ready for a story?***
Team A: ***No! Guess our category!***

Team A then begins acting out their charades while team B tries to guess what the category is. Any member of team B can guess, and the spokesperson for team A answers either yes or no. If the correct guess is made, team B tries to tag players from team A as they race to the opposite end of the playing area. If someone is tagged, he joins the other team. If a guess is not made in five tries, team A scores one point, and play begins again with team B acting out a category. Use the following category suggestions, then make up more of your own!

- animals
- kinds of food or eating
- emotions we might feel
- jobs people might have

- shapes
- tools
- musical instruments

 # CROSS THE RIVER
This lively outdoor game is sure to be a favorite!

Whatcha Need: You'll need six paper plates or cups and two 10-foot lengths of rope or crepe paper. (Use stones to hold crepe paper in place on the ground.)

Whatcha Do: Place the ropes or crepe-paper streamers at opposite ends of the playing field and about fifty feet apart. The area between the lines is the "river." Scatter the plastic cups or plates around the river, between the lines. Form two teams and have each team stand on lines opposite one another. Explain that in this game there are choices to make. Players can choose to simply cross the river to the other side without being tagged, and score one point for their team, or they may choose to try and pick up an item and cross the river without being tagged to score five points for their team. One team at a time crosses the river while the other team tries to tag runners. Begin by having the tag team shout: "If you shake or if you shiver, choose or lose and cross the river!" Then the opposite team runs to cross the river. If someone is tagged, she must freeze in place until everyone is across to the other line, then join the other team. Tally up the points after each crossing, then have the other team become the runners. Play until one team has lost its players or until one team scores fifty points.

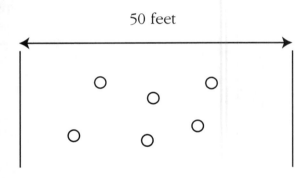

50 feet

 # LIFEBOATS AFLOAT
A fast-paced game of quick thinking and acting.

Whatcha Need: You'll need paper plates and a dice or number cube. (Power Hint: If you would like to make a number cube, simply cover a box with construction paper and number the sides. Roll the cube as you would a dice cube.)

Whatcha Do: Gather kids at one end of the room and hand each person a paper plate. Explain that in this game the paper plates are small lifeboats. You will roll a number to begin the game, and kids must race to form lifeboats with the same number of people as shown on the dice. This takes a bit of strategy! Some kids may just hold their paper plates and join someone else's boat, or they may have to use their boat for other players to hop in. For example, if number three is rolled, kids must form groups of three people all with one foot on one lifeboat. Each time a lifeboat with the correct number of people is formed, those players give each other high fives. If there are kids left off of a boat, they must remain seated until the next number is rolled, then race to join or form another boat. Play until every number has been rolled at least one time.

GET OFF MY BACK
A guessing game that doubles as a fun icebreaker.

Whatcha Need: You'll need index cards, markers, and a variety of "character" stickers such as nursery-rhyme characters, animals, storybook characters, Bible characters, or insects.

<table>
<tr><td>

Whatcha Know!

This game is especially fun at family picnics and for VBS activities! Or invite another class to get to know your class even better—and to share some fun and laughter.

</td><td>

Whatcha Do: Place a sticker on children's backs without letting them see what the pictures are of. Give kids a hint by telling them the category of the stickers, such as "insects." Then allow five minutes for kids to walk around the room asking yes or no questions that help them figure out who or what is on their backs. Questions might include: "Can I fly?" "Do I have legs?" "Are you afraid of me?" "Do I make you itch?" or "Am I beautiful?" When five minutes are up, have kids sit in a circle and let each child tell who he thinks is on his back. If correct, the child places his sticker on an index card to keep as a bookmark (and use to add other stickers too during additional rounds of the game). If the child cannot figure out who is on his back, have the rest of the kids act out the picture. When the child guesses correctly, add the picture to an index card. (Be sure to have kids write their names on their index cards.)

</td></tr>
</table>

BANANA-BANNA OLYMPICS
Goofy fun for a hot summer's day!

Whatcha Need: You'll need bananas, paper plates, and three boxes of fruit-flavored gelatin in different flavors.

Whatcha Do: Plan on staging this fruity Olympics event outdoors. Give each person a banana (peel on) and explain that in this series of lively events kids will use their bananas to compete against themselves and each other. Set two paper plates at each end of the playing area and about 20 feet apart. (You can reconfigure the paper plates or add more of them to use as obstacles, bases, or whatever else you may need for the various events.) Use the following events and score one point for each person finishing the event, two points for each person who finishes first in each.

EVENT 1: BANANA HOP. Place your banana under your chin and hop on one leg from one paper plate to the next and back again.

EVENT 2: BANANA BACK-UP. Place the banana on your back and walk backwards around a series of five paper plates and back again.

EVENT 3: BANANA TOSS. Get with partners and toss your bananas back and forth down the field, then return to the starting place.

EVENT 4: BANANA ROLL. Roll your banana around a circle of paper plates, then roll over the top of your banana without squishing it.

EVENT 5: BANANA FROGS. Partners leapfrog over each other while holding their bananas under their chins. Go from one end of the playing area to the other and back again.

When all the events have been completed, add up the scores. The kids with the highest scores may choose first which gelatin they would like sprinkled on clean paper plates to dip their bananas in and enjoy eating!

25 ROCKET BALL
A high-flying game that's perfect for outdoor fun!

Whatcha Need: You'll need a beach towel, a tennis ball, and three bases (such as towels, boxes, or plastic plates).

Whatcha Do: Set up the playing field as in the diagram, placing the bases at least 25 feet apart. Form two teams. Designate one team the first outfielders and have them get with partners. Partners must link elbows and not let them go during the time they are in the outfield. The other team will stand by home base and choose one player to be the first runner while the others hold the edges of a beach towel. Place a tennis ball on the towel, and have kids vault the ball high in the air and out to the outfield. The runner then tries to run as many bases as she can, but if the partners in the outfield catch the ball the runner is out. She then goes to hold the beach towel, and another player becomes the next runner. Score one point each time a runner crosses home base. Change sides when there are four outs on a team. Continue playing for five innings. The team with the highest number of runs is the winning team and can line up first for drinks of water.

Base 2

Base 1

Home
Base

MORE

GOODIES GALORE

Cinnamon snails, cool cracker candy, super fruit soup, and "munch" more are recipes for classroom cooperation and lip-smakin' fun!

A Bit of Background

Add a classroom full of kids, a pound of learning, a dash of tasty food, and a pinch of frolic, and what do you have? A winning recipe for classroom fun! And it's the kind of delicious fun your kids can't wait to sink their teeth into. Kids and cooking go together like cookies and milk! Cooking experiences and snack preparation are a great alternative to classroom crafts and make any Sunday school program or VBS more exciting and motivating. Plus, kids can learn a lot from the simplest of snack preparations, including:

- following directions,
- teamwork,
- working toward a cooperative goal, and
- responsibility for cleaning up.

Great goodies are as fun to make as they are to eat. Look for recipes that use age-appropriate tools and steer clear of sharp knives or metal graters that can be safety hazards. Fruits and vegetables lend themselves perfectly to yogurt-based dips and spreads—and kids love the creamy crunch! Cheeses and cold cuts look super when cut with cookie cutters and are layered on crackers or flour tortillas. Use pretzel sticks instead of toothpicks to make crazy fruit kabobs or edible sculptures.

Your kids may enjoy compiling a classroom recipe book of their favorite shared treats. Simply write the recipe and directions on copy paper, let kids draw pictures around the edges, then copy them off. Be sure to make a copy of the booklet for each child to take home—and many more to use as a service project with proceeds going to a local food shelter!

Keep in mind these quick-n-easy cooking tips.

✳ **For quick hand cleaning, provide baby wipes or other damp towelettes.**

✳ **Let kids make quick aprons by stapling several layers of paper towel to 3-foot lengths of black ribbon. Tie on the aprons, then simply tear off sheets of toweling when they become messy.**

✳ **Always check for allergies kids may have. Chocolate and nuts are often two problem foods. Substitute carob for chocolate and crispy rice cereal for nuts if needed.**

CINNAMON SNAILS

Whatcha Need: You'll need sliced wheat bread, spreadable margarine, cinnamon sugar, plastic knives, pretzel sticks, and paper towels.

Whatcha Do: Hand each person a paper towel, plastic knife, and a slice of wheat bread. Show kids how to cut the crusts from the bread and set the crusts aside. Spread softened margarine on the wheat bread, then sprinkle it with cinnamon sugar. Roll up the bread and gently cut it in half widthwise to make two "snails." Secure the snails so they don't unwind by poking two pretzel-stick "antennas" through each snail. Place the snails on paper towels and wrap the bread crusts around the bases of the snails for the ground. Snails may be slow, but kids' snacks will be gobbled up quickly! For even more fun and color, sprinkle chocolate shavings or green decorator sugar over the margarine!

Here's a tasty variation that calls for a toaster oven. Spread softened cream cheese on the bread, then sprinkle with cinnamon sugar. Secure snails with toothpicks, then drizzle melted margarine over them and dip into cinnamon sugar. Bake for twelve minutes at 350 degrees, then cool and enjoy!

PEANUT CHIP ROLL-UPS

Whatcha Need: You'll need flour tortillas, paper towels, plastic knives, crunchy peanut butter, mini chocolate chips (or Nutella spreadable nutty chocolate; beside the peanut butter at grocery stores).

Whatcha Do: Distribute paper towels or napkins and plastic knives. Hand each child a flour tortilla and have kids spread peanut butter over the tortilla. Sprinkle the peanut butter with chocolate chips (or spread on the Nutella … mmm), then roll up and enjoy. Consider making several of these sweet treats and sharing them with another class, or have kids cut the treats into 3-inch portions and place on decorated paper plates to hand out after the adult worship services are over!

PUMPKIN SMOOTHIES

Whatcha Need: You'll need self-sealing sandwich bags (like zipper-lock bags), plastic spoons, nutmeg, canned pumpkin (one can for every six kids), cinnamon, a measuring cup, and one can of evaporated milk.

Whatcha Do: Hand each person a plastic spoon and a self-sealing sandwich bag. Have each person use a plastic spoon to measure the following ingredients into the bag: ⅓ spoon of nutmeg, ⅓ spoon of cinnamon, and 5 spoons of evaporated milk. To each bag, add ½ cup of canned pumpkin. Seal the sandwich bags and have kids smush the contents gently. When the ingredients look well mixed, open the bags and spoon out the goodies. This is a perfect snack for Thanksgiving time or when studying about the harvest and Feast of Tents!

For pumpkin pie in a bag, simply crumble a graham cracker into the bag after mashing the ingredients. Or try adding a dollop of whipped topping to the mixed ingredients and graham crackers.

SOUP-CAN BREAD

Whatcha Need: You'll need several tubes of refrigerator French bread dough (a tube for every three to four kids); nonstick cooking spray; a knife; clean, empty soup cans (for each person and without labels); cookie sheets; a can opener; and access to an oven. (Hint: This is a nifty idea, and even though it takes a few minutes to bake the bread, it's worth the wait!)

Whatcha Do: Preheat your oven according to the directions on the tubes of bread dough. Open the tubes and divide the bread dough into three or four portions. Hand a clean, empty soup can and a portion of dough to each child. Have kids spray the insides of their soup cans using the nonstick cooking spray. Let kids gently knead the dough for about thirty seconds, then roll the dough into shapes that will fit in the soup cans. After the dough is in the cans, stand the cans, open sides up, on a cookie sheet and carefully place the cookie sheet in the heated oven.

Bake the bread according to the directions on the bread-dough tubes or until the loaves peek over the tops of the cans and look golden brown. Cool the bread in the cans for about ten minutes, then use a knife to loosen the loaves and remove the bread when it is completely cooled. (You may need to open the other end of a can that is being stubborn!)

> ## Whatcha Know!
>
> Mix softened margarine and honey and spread on the warm loaves of bread. Or have kids simply dip pieces of their fresh bread into a bowl of honey. What a great idea to use with Jesus as the bread of life!

 # SNICKER SALAD

Whatcha Need: You'll need sliced apples, plastic forks and knives, bananas, bite-sized Snickers candy pieces, paper bowls, and whipped topping (if desired).

Whatcha Do: Distribute the paper bowls, plastic forks, and knives. Let kids chop several apple slices into their bowls and add half a sliced banana to the apples. Chop a bite-sized Snickers bar or cube and sprinkle it over the fruit. Finally, add a dollop of whipped topping if desired. Yum! Try one of these fast-n-easy variations for great party goodies:

• Hollow out the insides of small apples. Chop the insides of apples with pineapple bits and bananas. Mix the fruit in a few spoonfuls of whipped topping and replace in the hollow apple. Sprinkle the tops of your fruit bowls with coconut or dried fruit bits.

• Make one peel on a small banana and hollow out a place in the fruit. Fill the banana with mashed banana, chopped pineapple bits, and chopped Snickers bars. Fold the peel back over the opening and place on a cookie sheet. Bake for ten minutes at 350 degrees. Cool and enjoy!

 # SALAD SACKS

Whatcha Need: You'll need self-sealing sandwich bags, plastic forks and spoons, sugar, lemon juice, chow-mein noodles or sunflower seeds (hulled), and the following fresh vegetables: lettuce, spinach leaves, shredded carrots, and broccoli bits. (Hint: Instead of lemon and sugar, you could provide ready-made salad dressings such as Ranch and French.)

Whatcha Do: Invite kids to help clean and prepare the fresh vegetables. Then hand each person a self-sealing sandwich bag and let kids add their favorite salad vegetables. Then have kids each add 1 spoonful of sugar and 3 spoonfuls of lemon juice to their sandwich bags. (Add salad dressing if you're using that instead of lemon and sugar.) Seal the bag tightly, then shake the bags in all directions to coat the vegetables. Finally, open the salad sacks, sprinkle on chow-mein noodles and enjoy right from the sacks!

For another fun twist, set up a "salad bar" and include the following tidbits to add to your salad sacks:

- shredded cheese
- raisins or dried fruits
- fresh mushrooms
- pepperoni bits
- small crackers
- frozen peas

BACON 'N EGGS CANDY

Whatcha Need: You'll need paper plates, plastic spoons, pretzel sticks, a bowl of melted white chocolate or white candy coating, and yellow M&M candies (or small lemon or butterscotch disks).

Whatcha Do: Hand each person a paper plate on which to make a bacon 'n eggs treat. Show kids how to lay three or four pretzel-stick "bacon strips" side by side on a plate. Plop a small spoonful of melted white chocolate or white candy coating in the center to hold the pretzels together and to form the "egg white." Place a yellow M&M (or butterscotch disk) in the center of the white chocolate to make the yolk. Let the treats harden at room temperature for about ten minutes before nibbling. (Or place the treats in a refrigerator for five minutes to harden them.)

FLOWER POWER!

Whatcha Need: You'll need canned white icing, food coloring, plastic self-sealing sandwich bags (two for every person), plastic spoons, paper towels, scissors, and a box of round crackers or small round cookies (such as chocolate or vanilla wafer-type cookies) to decorate.

Whatcha Do: This snack idea is great for a quick treat when learning about how God created the world. Have kids find partners or form trios. Hand each person two sandwich bags, at least two cookies or crackers, and a paper towel. Explain that you'll be creating delicious, edible flowers using the sandwich bags as squeezy icing tubes. Encourage kids to choose their colors before beginning. Each child may want to make a different color of icing so there are more colors to share between partners!) Scoop two spoonfuls of canned icing into each sandwich bag, then add several drops of food coloring. Seal the bags and squish the icing to color it uniformly. Then snip a bottom corner from each bag. Squeeze the icing into swirls, lines, rosettes, and dots on the cracker or cookie flowers to decorate them. As you nibble your awesome edibles, name parts of God's creation that are your favorites. For a fun twist with younger kids, try decorating insects instead of flowers. Ladybugs and bumble bees are especially cute!

 # BANANA BLASTERS

Whatcha Need: You'll need paper plates, new craft sticks, banana halves, honey, and wheat germ, oatmeal, or granola.

Whatcha Do: Hand each person a paper plate and a banana half. Pour honey onto a paper plate and wheat germ, oatmeal, or granola onto another plate. Have kids peel their banana halves and poke craft sticks in the bananas on the flat side. Roll the bananas in honey until they're fully coated. Then roll the banana blasters in wheat germ, oatmeal, or granola. Kids will skyrocket over the taste!

 # CHILI DILLY DIP

Whatcha Need: You'll need ½ cup shredded cheddar cheese, a can of chili with beans, a small package of cream cheese, corn chips, paper cups, plastic spoons, a mixing spoon, and an electric skillet. (Hint: This recipe serves ten to twelve kids.)

Whatcha Do: Have kids help mix a can of chili and a package of cream cheese in an electric skillet. Turn the skillet on medium and let kids take turns stirring the mixture until the cream cheese is melted and the ingredients are thoroughly mixed. When the mixture is hot, turn off the heat and sprinkle ½ cup shredded cheddar cheese over the chili cheese. Spoon the dip into paper cups. Fill a plastic bowl with crispy corn chips for dipping, or spoon a bit of dip onto each chip.

Try these yummy variations for even more south-of-the border flavor!
- Add chopped olives to the chili-cheese mixture.
- Spoon the dip into taco shells and add shredded lettuce and tomato bits on top.
- Make a double or triple batch of the dip and serve it in small bowls with corn chips crumbled on top as a treat for the whole church!

 # NEAT-O NACHOS!

Whatcha Need: You'll need aluminum foil, cinnamon sugar, flour tortillas, melted margarine, plastic spoons and knives, paper plates, cookie sheets, a bowl of white icing (thinned with a bit of water), paper lunch sacks, access to an oven or large toaster oven, clean scissors, grape halves, and green, dried fruit roll-ups.

Whatcha Do: Preheat the oven to 375 degrees. Set out the ingredients in four assembly-line stations as follows: station one needs plastic knives and flour tortillas; station two needs melted margarine and cinnamon sugar in paper lunch sacks; station three needs aluminum foil and cookie sheets; and station four needs clean scissors and green fruit roll-ups. Have kids form four groups, then designate the groups as follows: the Chippers (go to station one), the Snippers (go to station four), the Shakers (go to station two), and the Bakers (go to station three). Have each group perform the following cooking jobs.

Chippers: Cut flour tortillas into pie-shaped wedges, six wedges per tortilla.

Snippers: Snip green fruit roll-ups into shreds of "lettuce" (set aside).

Shakers: Drizzle melted margarine over the tortilla wedges, then shake in cinnamon sugar in paper lunch sacks.

Bakers: Place the cinnamon-coated tortilla wedges on foil-covered cookie sheets in single layers.

Bake the cinnamon-coated tortilla wedges in an oven for twelve minutes. Remove the tortillas from the oven and cool. Top with shredded lettuce (green roll-ups), green olives (grape halves), and drizzle with sour cream (white icing). Mmm—whatta treat!

PIZZA SALADS

Whatcha Need: You'll need small cardboard pizza rounds (from most pizza shops for free), ready-made salad mix (lettuce, carrots, and all in the mix), a can of drained garbanzo beans, chopped olives, small tomatoes (sliced), shredded cheeses (mozzarella and cheddar), pepperoni slices, Ranch dressing, and plastic forks.

Whatcha Do: If you can't find cardboard pizza rounds, simply use small plastic or paper plates (red ones are especially nice). Set out the ingredients assembly-line style and let kids assemble their pizza salads layer by layer. First add a layer of salad greens and carrots for the pizza "crusts." Then top the pizzas with slices of pepperoni, tomatoes, olives, garbanzo beans, and shredded cheeses. Finally, drizzle Ranch dressing over the ingredients as "pizza sauce." This fun-to-assemble salad is healthy, colorful, and makes a perfect nonsweet snack for VBS or children's church.

ASTRONAUT PUDDING

Whatcha Need: You'll need self-sealing sandwich bags, instant pudding in a variety of flavors (chocolate, vanilla, and strawberry are best), evaporated milk (or regular milk), measuring cups and spoons, and plastic drinking straws.

Whatcha Do: Distribute the self-sealing sandwich bags and plastic drinking straws. Have kids each measure 2 tablespoons of instant pudding into their bags along with ½ cup of evaporated (or regular) milk. Seal the bag securely, then squish the pudding mix and milk together so it's smooth. Wait one minute to let the mixture thicken, then slightly open the bags and stick plastic straws in to sip out the pudding. No fuss to make—no mess to clean up!

Try one of these neat ideas to make astronaut pudding even more fun!

• Make vanilla pudding and add a few drops of blue food coloring to each bag before mixing.

• Stir in small candy sprinkles to make sparkly asteroids and stars.

• Decorate the sandwich bags with star stickers, then take your unusual treats to another class as an awesome act of kindness!

# 'NANNER DOGS

Whatcha Need: You'll need small bananas (one per person), hot-dog buns, paper plates, peanut butter, chocolate syrup, pineapple bits, mini marshmallows, and plastic spoons and knives.

Whatcha Do: Kids will love these portable banana splits! Distribute the bananas, hot-dog buns, and paper plates. Have kids spread peanut butter on the insides of the hot-dog buns. Peel the bananas and place them in the buns. Drizzle on chocolate-syrup "ketchup," then add mini marshmallow "onions" and pineapple bits as "relish." For younger kids, try slicing the bananas on the buns and calling these goodies banana boats.

# SUNRISE ON THE MOUNTAINS

Whatcha Need: You'll need clear plastic drinking glasses, vanilla ice cream, measuring cups and spoons, frozen orange-juice concentrate, a pitcher, water, chocolate syrup, and plastic spoons.

Whatcha Do: This chilly, willy treat is perfect for summertime programs, family picnics, and VBS! Prepare the frozen orange-juice concentrate, but add only a can and a half of cold water. (You want the concentrate to be rather thick.) Hand each person a clear plastic drinking glass and plastic spoon. For each Sunrise on the Mountains drink, simply add ½ cup of vanilla ice cream to the glass and top it with ¼ cup of orange juice and 2 tablespoons of chocolate syrup. Let kids scoop the goodies out using their plastic spoons. It's delicious, nutritious, and so beautiful in the cups!

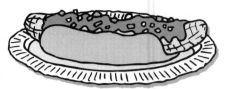
Whatcha Know!

Try other flavors of juice, substituting them for the prepared orange juice, or replace the vanilla ice cream with sherbet or sorbet for another fruity, tasty twist.

HARVEST POCKETS

Whatcha Need: You'll need shredded vegetable slaw mix (either cabbage or broccoli slaw), mixing bowls and spoons, two cartons of vanilla yogurt, honey, plastic forks, slivered almonds, paper towels, and a pita pocket for each person.

Whatcha Do: This is a wonderful snack idea to use when learning about the harvest, firstfruits, or the land of "milk and honey." Have kids help empty a package of vegetable slaw into one mixing bowl and the yogurt into another mixing bowl. Add one mixing spoon of honey to the yogurt and stir to mix it thoroughly. Distribute the pita pockets and let kids spoon vegetable slaw into the pockets. Drizzle the milk-n-honey yogurt mixture over the vegetables, add almonds for topping, then nibble and enjoy! For more taste treats that parallel the harvest, add one or more of the following toppings:
- raisins
- granola
- chopped olives
- chopped dates
- square corn cereal
- shredded cheese

SNACK SACKS

Whatcha Need: You'll need graham crackers, a carton of spreadable cream cheese (for every eight kids), plastic spoons, paper towels, self-sealing sandwich bags, and fruit preserves in strawberry, blueberry, or other flavors.

Whatcha Do: Hand each person a graham cracker and a self-sealing sandwich bag. Have kids seal their bags, then crush the graham crackers. Carefully empty the crushed crackers on paper towels and set them aside for a moment. In each sandwich bag, add four plastic spoonfuls of softened cream cheese and two spoonfuls of fruit preserves. Have kids seal the bags tightly and squish the cream cheese and preserves until they're well mixed. Open the bags and sprinkle the crushed graham crackers over the cream-cheese mixture, then use plastic spoons to dig in and enjoy. If there are extra graham crackers, kids might enjoy spreading the cream-cheese mixture over the crackers.

CORN CHIPS

Whatcha Need: You'll need paper towels, cornmeal, vegetable oil, salt, water, measuring cups and spoons, a large bowl and mixing spoon, cookie sheets, a bowl of salsa, plastic spoons, and access to an oven (or large toaster oven or electric skillet). (Hint: A regular oven will work best, but you can use a large toaster oven or electric skillet and plan to do several batches of chips.)

Whatcha Do: Preheat the oven to 400 degrees and pour 2 tablespoons of vegetable oil on a cookie sheet. Have kids form two groups: the measurers and the chippers. Have the measurers measure the following ingredients into a large mixing bowl: 1 cup of cornmeal, ½ teaspoon of salt, 1½ tablespoons of vegetable oil, and ¾ cup of very hot water. Mix the ingredients well. Then have the chippers place small spoonfuls (use plastic spoons) of the chip mixture on the cookie sheets and use their fingers to pat and gently press each chip so it's very thin.

Make as many chips as the mixture allows (approximately twenty chips). Be sure the chips have plenty of oil surrounding them or they will stick when heated. Place the cookie sheet in the heated oven for about 10 minutes or until the chips look crisp and golden brown. Place the hot chips on paper towels to absorb excess grease and cool. Then salt them lightly and dip in salsa to enjoy. (If you're using an electric skillet, heat the chips in oil at 400 degrees for ten to twelve minutes or until crisp and brown.) Try grating cheddar cheese over your chips while they're warm for an extra taste treat!

OLLIE OWLS

Whatcha Need: You'll need rice cakes, peanut butter, fruit cereal loops, raisins, American cheese slices, bananas, plastic knives, and paper towels or plates.

Whatcha Do: Hand each person a rice cake, a plastic knife, and a paper towel or paper plate. Have kids spread peanut butter over the tops of the rice cakes. Add sliced bananas for the eyes and place a raisin in the center of each banana slice for the eye balls. Place three fruit cereal loops above each eye for the brows, and cut triangle-shaped "beaks" from the American cheese slices. Young kids especially enjoy assembling these cute owls, and they make a fun accompaniment to lessons about why being wise through God's help is important.

20 SMILIN' FACES

Whatcha Need: You'll need one refrigerator biscuit per person, apple slices, raisins, small marshmallows, aluminum foil, cookie sheets, chocolate kisses, and a large toaster oven or regular oven.

Whatcha Do: These funny faces are a favorite with kids of all ages! Preheat the oven to 350 degrees. For each smilin' face, place a biscuit-dough biscuit on a small square of foil. Place two apple-slice "lips" on the biscuit with the red peel pointing outward and the white apple portion stuck in the dough. (Slightly spread the slices, as you'll stick marshmallow "teeth" in between them after cooking the biscuits.) Add raisins for eyes and a chocolate candy kiss for a funny nose. Bake the biscuits at 350 degrees for about eight minutes or until they're a light, golden brown. After cooling for a few minutes, add small marshmallow "teeth" between the smiling lips.

21 CRACKER CANDY

Whatcha Need: You'll need a box of soda or saltine crackers, a small bag of chocolate chips (semi-sweet or milk chocolate), 1 cup of margarine, 1 cup of brown sugar, 1 cup of crushed peanuts (optional), paper plates, a mixing spoon, and an electric skillet.

Whatcha Do: Have kids help with the simple preparation of this yummy—and very unusual—candy treat. Warm the electric skillet on medium and let kids place in the skillet the following ingredients: a cup of margarine, a bag of chocolate chips, a cup of brown sugar, and a cup of crushed peanuts (if you desire). Take turns stirring the mixture until the margarine and chocolate chips are melted together with the sugar and the mixture is bubbly and smooth. Turn off the heat and have kids place several soda crackers on their paper plates. Carefully drizzle the candy mixture over the crackers and enjoy.

Whatcha Know!

Prepare small plastic plates of these yummy crackers to present to people who are recovering from an illness or who need a sweet reminder that they're loved! Refrigerate the cracker candies for 10 minutes, then cover the plates with plastic wrap and add colorful bows on top.

FRUIT SOUP

Whatcha Need: You'll need a large mixing spoon and bowl or pot, melon without the rinds (honeydew and cantaloupe), bananas, grapes, one can of frozen orange-juice concentrate, two cartons of strawberry yogurt, plastic knives, paper cups, a ladle, and a 32-ounce bottle of apple juice.

Whatcha Do: This recipe will make enough fruit soup for ten to twelve kids. Have kids cut the fruit into small cubes, slices, and pieces. Place the fruit in the large mixing bowl or pot. Add the can of frozen orange juice concentrate, the strawberry yogurt, and the bottle of apple juice. Stir the ingredients well, then ladle into paper cups to enjoy.

For extra tasty twists, try one of these ideas.
- Add a bottle of sugar-free lemon-line soda to your soup.
- Make Hawaiian fruit soup and add pineapple tidbits and coconut shreds.
- Cut fresh oranges in half and hollow out the fruit. Add the fresh oranges to your fruit soup, then ladle the soup into the orange-peel bowls.
- For a frosty twist, add a scoop of sherbet or sorbet to each soup bowl.

SCENIC SNACKS

Whatcha Need: You'll need plastic plates, blue gelatin (prepared or ready made), striped sticks of gum, candy gummy fish, vanilla cookies (wafer type), and plastic spoons.

Whatcha Do: Hand each person a plastic plate. Show kids how to crush vanilla cookies to make sand on one side of their plates as the "beach." Spoon blue gelatin onto the other half of the plates as the "ocean." Remove the gum wrappers and place sticks of gum on the beach as striped "beach towels." Finally, add several gummy fish to the water. What a fun summertime treat! Just think of all the extras you could add: peanut "sunbathers" or "boats," marshmallow "sand castles," or even lifesavers on the water!

MATZOS AND CLOTHS

Whatcha Need: You'll need a box of matzo crackers, softened cream cheese, honey, permanent markers, small plastic plates, and a white men's handkerchief for each child. (Hint: This is a craft and edible idea all in one!)

Whatcha Do: Explain to kids the significance of Passover and how the Hebrews left Egypt so quickly that they had no time to let their bread rise. Their bread was dried and very flat but lasted well on their long escape and travels. The flat bread was covered with cloths to keep the dust off of it and to help it stay a bit fresher. The bread was called "matzo" (hold up a matzo cracker) and is still eaten at Passover celebrations today. Have kids make matzo cloths by using permanent markers to decorate the white handkerchiefs. When the cloths are finished, place several matzo crackers on small plastic plates and cover them with the matzo cloths. Offer a prayer thanking God for giving us good foods to eat, then remove the covers and enjoy your matzos with cream cheese and honey.

25 BIRD NESTS

Whatcha Need: You'll need small doughnuts, paper towels, plastic knives, canned chocolate icing (or peanut butter), chow-mein noodles, and jelly beans.

Whatcha Do: This is a festive springtime treat kids love to make and eat! Have kids ice the tops of their doughnuts with canned chocolate icing or peanut butter. Use chow-mein noodles to cover the icing, then add several "bird's egg" jelly beans to the top. If it's close to Easter, you may wish to let kids add a marshmallow chick to the nest!

Whatcha Know!

Bird-nest doughnuts are fun for kids to serve the congregation after morning church services. Serve the nests on large platters or cookie sheets covered with brown construction-paper strips to resemble nests. Add napkins, tea, and chilled juice to round out your morning fellowship time!

MORE

PRAYER & WORSHIP

Creative prayers and worship activities to encourage kids to deepen their faith as they draw nearer to God!

A Bit of Background

Prayer and worship are natural and necessary parts of any children's Christian-education program. Still, although they are essential, they're not always easy to teach in creative ways. Some people think of prayer as some inborn ability not requiring formal or creative instruction. But just as Jesus taught his followers to pray in Luke 11:1-4, children need instruction in effective, powerful prayer, too. Inspire prayer confidence in kids by assuring them that God doesn't mind how we pray—whether it's kneeling, sitting, standing, or laying—and that God doesn't care if we choose to pray silently or aloud, alone or with others. Help kids realize that God created us individually and that we all have unique and individual ways to express ourselves through prayer and worship. It's not the *how* that matters as much as they *why* and *when*!

Help kids learn to draw nearer to God through prayer and worship by allowing them freedom of expression. Try partner prayers and small-group worship or see what kids can do with pantomime or sign language. Share worship songs and poems written by kids or let them express musical prayers by playing simple rhythm instruments. Never force a shy child to pray or worship aloud if he feels uncomfortable. Instead, offer partner and small-group experiences to build his confidence and reassure shy kids that God hears and delights in them whether their prayers or praise are silent or aloud. Here are some other important reminders to pass along to kids as they explore their prayer and praise lives.

✴ ***God answers faithful prayers.*** (Mark 11:24)

✴ ***We can pray for others any time or place.*** (Colossians 1:9)

✴ ***We're to pray in Jesus' name.*** (John 14:13)

✴ ***God always listens to our prayers.*** (Proverbs 15:29b)

As you explore prayer and worship with your kids and encourage them to draw nearer to God through their sincere expressions of love and praise, guide them to recognize that prayer and worship are two of the most joy-filled ways we express our love to God. And always remember that your own modeling of prayer and worship can lead kids in an ever-deepening relationship with our heavenly Father as they build a prayerful, powerful, worshipful lifestyle that will last a lifetime and beyond!

WELCOME TO WORSHIP

Welcoming others to worship
Romans 16:16

Whatcha Need: You'll need a Bible, a stapler, scissors, fine-tipped permanent markers, ½-inch wide purple ribbon, and chocolate candy kisses.

Whatcha Do: Explain that according to the New Testament there were many new Christians who came together to worship, praise, and pray. Read aloud Romans 16:16, then tell kids that Paul meant we are to greet one another purely and sweetly and encourage others to share in worshiping the Lord. Tell kids you can worship God by helping welcome others into his house. Cut purple ribbon into 6-inch lengths and write "Welcome to worship!" on the ribbons using fine-tipped permanent mark-  ers. Then staple the greeting ribbons to the foil tops of chocolate candy kisses. Plan on having kids greet worshipers as they enter the church with a hug and their own version of sweet, holy kisses.

WORSHIP WORDS

Learning God's Word as a way to worship
Psalms 100; 105:1-5; 117

Whatcha Need: You'll need a Bible, three large sheets of poster board, and black and red markers.

Whatcha Do: Form three groups and hand each a black marker and a large sheet of poster board. Be sure each group has a Bible. Assign each group one of the following Psalms (or portions of Scripture): Psalm 100; Psalm 105:1-5; and Psalm 117. Explain that the book of Psalms in the Bible is a book filled with worshipful prayers and praises to God. The writers of the various psalms spoke to God through their words—sometimes in prayer, sometimes in songs, but always with attitudes of worship. Tell kids to write their assigned verses or psalms on the poster board using black marker. Then explain you'll go on a wor-ship-word safari and try to identify words of worship in each other's psalms. When the psalms are written on the poster board, have kids take turns reading the psalms aloud and identifying worship words and phrases such as "glorify," "honor," "praise," "come before him," and so on. Use red markers to circle the words and phrases. Then have kids turn their posters over and compose a short psalm of worship to God using some of the words they identified.

RAISE YOUR PRAISE

Praising and worshiping God with our voices
2 Samuel 22:1-4; Psalm 9:2

Whatcha Need: You'll need a Bible, black construction paper, scissors, glue sticks, and copies of the Song Sagas from page 50.

Whatcha Do: Before class, cut out simple music notes to hang on the wall as samples. If you prefer, consider making traceable patterns of music notes from old file folders. Be sure to make the patterns large enough to hold a copy of the Song Saga cards. (Include pencils to the supply list if you make patterns for kids to trace.) Gather kids and ask them to name their favorite ways to praise the Lord. Is it through reading the Bible or writing poems to God? Or do they prefer to praise and worship God through quiet prayer or joyous singing? Remind kids that there are many ways to worship and praise God and any way we choose to express ourselves is a demonstration of our love of the Lord. Tell kids that as long as people have had voices, they have sung songs to honor God. Remind kids that David lifted his voice in song many times to worship and thank God for his wondrous deeds and help. Invite volunteers to read aloud 2 Samuel 22:1-4 and Psalm 9:2.

Explain that many worship songs we sing today were written years ago and have interesting stories of how they were written. Distribute the Song Saga copies and read each aloud, then sing a few lines from each song. Explain that you can serve the whole congregation by helping them learn about worship songs. Hand out black construction paper and have kids cut out musical notes. Glue one song saga to each musical note, then either hand out the musical notes before worship (and plan on singing these songs during the service) or display the musical notes on a wall where everyone can read and enjoy them.

SONG SAGAS

JESUS LOVES ME

This favorite worship song was composed in 1859 by Anna Warner. Anna loved teaching Sunday school to army officers at West Point and wanted to teach the soldiers about the depth of Jesus' love for them.

AMAZING GRACE

John Newton was the owner of a slave ship who did not know Jesus until a violent storm at sea changed his mind—and heart. In 1779 Newton wrote *Amazing Grace* as a joyous expression of the grace that had saved his life.

SILENT NIGHT

In 1818, Franz Gruber wrote *Silent Night,* which soon became our most beloved worship song of Christmas. Gruber was to perform his new piece on the organ on Christmas Eve but found it truly silent—and instead played his guitar to worship Jesus.

ROCK OF AGES

On a stormy night in 1775, Augustus Toplady found a safe place in a crevice between two large rocks. Safe from the lightning, Toplady reflected on how God saves us in times of trouble. During that raging storm Toplady penned the opening lines of this classic song.

MEET OUR MINISTER!
Meeting the worship leaders in your church
1 Timothy 5:17

Whatcha Need: You'll need balloons, index cards or 3-by-5-inch construction-paper cards, permanent markers, markers, scissors, a stapler, and ribbon.

Whatcha Do: This activity will help kids connect with your church leadership or worship team and vice versa. Before the activity, choose someone you would like to get to know better, such as the minister, music or choir leader, children's pastor, youth leader, or other members of your worship team. Then have kids inflate and knot their balloons. Invite kids to use permanent markers to sign their balloons and list some their own favorite things on the balloons. Suggestions might include their favorite colors, foods, pets, parts of God's creation, favorite part of church, or dreams they have for the future. On the index or construction-paper cards, have kids pose one question about worship for a church leader, such as, "Why do you like serving God?" or "What is your favorite way to worship God?" (Be sure the leader includes his or her own card!) Tie a 3-foot length of ribbon to each balloon, then staple the question cards to the ribbons. Gather all of the balloons and cards into a bouquet and tie them together with a ribbon bow. Ask the person who receives the bouquet to jot down the answers to the kids' questions on the backs of the cards, then return the cards for kids to read aloud the next week.

Whatcha Know!

For an extra-special touch, use helium-filled balloons so your bouquet won't look "wilted." This worship activity is a wonderful encouragement to church leaders, so consider making a bouquet for a different church leader each month of the year!

PRAYER PROPS
Helping kids feel more comfortable praying
1 Timothy 2:8

Whatcha Need: You'll need a pretend microphone, a tape recorder and blank tape, a megaphone, and a nonworking phone.

Whatcha Do: Place each of the four items—the microphone, the phone, the tape recorder, and the megaphone—in a different corner of the room. Gather kids in the center of the room and ask them which of the four talking devices they'd feel most comfortable using if they were going to give a speech or talk in front of people. Have kids go stand by the device they would choose, then encourage kids to tell why they chose the devices they did.

After kids share their opinions, tell them that because we're all individuals we all have different ways of expressing ourselves. Some people are comfortable speaking out loud and having lots of people hear, while others are more shy and prefer a quieter way of expressing themselves to another person, such as through a telephone. Remind kids that as individuals we all have different ways and comfort levels of expressing our needs and wants to God through prayer. Some of us are comfortable praying with people, while others of us prefer quiet, alone prayers. Have kids think of a short prayer thanking God for giving us different ways to pray, then have kids use the devices they chose to pray. (The recorded prayers will be fun listening to later!) If there's time, invite kids to visit another corner and to try out a prayer using a different prayer prop. See if all the kids would like to record a familiar prayer such as the Lord's Prayer together and tape record it to play over the next few weeks before prayer time.

TOGETHER TRIANGLES
Gathering kids together in worship
Matthew 18:19, 20

Whatcha Need: You'll need poster board, tape, wallpaper samples, scissors, glue sticks, tape, and permanent markers.

Whatcha Do: You may wish to make a few 8-inch triangle patterns for kids to trace around on their poster board. Have kids each cut out a large poster-board triangle (at least 8-inches). Then cover the triangles with wallpaper by gluing the paper in place with glue sticks. Have kids write their names across the triangles, then work together to assemble the triangles on the wall to form God's name. As you work, remind kids that whenever we gather to pray or worship God, we gather in his name and become part of one body of worship. When the word "God" has been formed and taped in place, gather under the name for a prayer of thanks that God loves us and desires us to gather in his name as one body of believers.

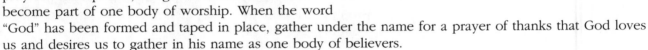

GREETING GOD
Ways to praise God
Luke 11:2

Whatcha Need: You'll need markers, index cards, and three paper lunch sacks.

Whatcha Do: Before this activity, write "Belonging Words" on one paper sack, "Describing Words" on a second sack, and "Names" on a third sack. Count out three index cards for the first sack, and on them write the following words, one per card: "My," "Our," and "Dear." Place them in the Belonging Words sack. Then write the following words on more index cards and slide them in sack two: "powerful," "awesome," "heavenly," "holy," "gracious," and "loving." For the Names sack, write the following words on index cards and place them in the sack: "Father," "God," "Lord," "Jesus," and "Holy One." Explain to kids that meeting and greeting the Lord is important in prayer and worship. Point out that most people seem to begin their prayers with the words, "Dear Father" or "Dear Lord" but that there are many more ways to honor and praise God as we meet and greet him! Have three volunteers pull a card from each sack and hold them in order of Belonging Word, Describing Word, and Name. Have the class read the words. For example, you may have as a greeting, "Our awesome God" or "My gracious Father." See how many combinations you can make, then have kids add more word cards to the sacks and continue meeting and greeting God in unique ways.

Older kids may enjoy adding a fourth sack titled "You Are Words" and containing cards that say, "You are our Creator" or "You are more powerful than anyone." Read these cards after the first three have been read, and you are on your way to a powerful prayer of worship!

SILENT AND STILL
Being still before God
Psalms 37:7; 46:10

Whatcha Need: You'll need pencils, white poster board, tape, scissors, and glow-in-the-dark markers. (A slightly darkened room will really make this activity glow!)

Whatcha Do: Have kids trace one of their hands on white poster board and cut it out. Use the paper hands to trace and cut out one more so each child has a pair of paper hands. Have kids lay the hands on the floor with thumbs together, then color the hands using glow-in-the-dark markers. When the hands are colored, tape them in place over the palms of your real hands. Have kids hold their paper hands up toward the light as you remind them that when we worship God we want to come before him with peaceful, quiet hearts so we can praise him and express our love fully. Being quiet and still before God is a way to worship him. Turn down the lights (so kids can still see you and so their paper hands slightly glow) and ask for a moment of silence and stillness. Then quietly lead kids in the following action prayer as they follow along in silence and pantomime.

> *Dear glorious Father in heaven,* (place hands on your hearts)
> *You are with us when the sun rises,* (raise hands upward)
> *And when the sun sets low in the sky.* (sweep hands along the floor)
> *You are with us all night as we sleep tight.* (lay head on hands)
> *You guide us in the right paths* (hold hands to the left, then right)
> *And are always there to comfort us.* (give yourself a hug)
> *You shower us with love and blessings.* (raise hands, then lower them)
> *We offer our love to you always.* (touch hearts, then raise hands upward)
> *Amen.* (place palms together)

LIGHT OF LOVE
Worship as an expression of our love for God
Romans 12:1

Whatcha Need: You'll need colorful candle-wax chips (from craft stores), toothpicks, aluminum foil, small pillar candles, and an electric skillet.

Whatcha Do: Line the electric skillet with foil, then set the heat on low and set the skillet out of reach of kids for now. Hand each person a small pillar candle and a toothpick. Ask kids what they say or do when someone does something wonderful or kind for them. After kids tell that they express their thanks or love, remind them that God is always blessing us, helping us, leading and guiding us, and showering us with his love. Explain that when we worship

God it is a way to express our thanks and love to and for God. Point out that candles are often used during worship to symbolize the Lord as our light in a dark world and also the light of love he shines in our lives. Explain that worshiping God not only lights up own hearts with love but also lights up God's heart as well.

Show kids how to stick toothpicks in candle-wax chips and hold them against the foil on the bottom of the electric skillet until the wax begins to melt. Quickly stick the melting wax chips to the sides of the pillar candles and count to five (to allow time for the wax to harden and the chip to stick to the candle). Continue placing mosaic piece of wax to the candles until they're decorated. Make candle holders from scrunched aluminum foil. Tell kids to have an adult light the candles at mealtimes or other times when they want to worship God by expressing their love and thanks.

 # ONE WORLD

God's control of everything
Psalm 95:4-6

Whatcha Need: You'll need a white balloon and colored permanent markers.

Whatcha Do: Before this activity, inflate and knot the balloon, then use markers to make the balloon look like a globe. Have kids form a small circle and ask them who is in control of things in the world such as rain, wind, the sunrise, clouds, flowers, and mountains. Remind kids that God created the world and that he has control of all things in the world. Tell kids we worship God because he is more powerful than anyone or anything and because he has ultimate control. Let kids bop the balloon back and forth around the circle. Each time they bop the balloon, have them name something God controls in the world. After everyone has had at least one turn, share a prayer thanking God for his control. Then bop the balloon around once more as you worship God by singing, "He's Got the Whole World in His Hands."

If there's time and you have enough balloons, invite kids to make their own balloon globes to remind them that we worship our God who is in control of everything. Write Psalm 95:6 on the balloons, then add ribbon ties to the knots.

 # WORSHIP WHO AND WHAT

Why we worship God
Nehemiah 9:5; Psalm 148:1-13

Whatcha Need: You'll need water-based markers, tape, a large sheet of poster board, and clear transparencies. (You may also wish to have an overhead projector handy.)

Whatcha Do: Write the words to the song from this activity on a large sheet of poster board and tape it to the wall. Then lead kids in singing the words to the tune of "Jesus Loves Me." After singing the song two times, visit about why we worship God, with an emphasis on worshiping God for who he is and for what he does. Then have kids find partners and draw with markers on the clear transparencies scenes and pictures that express their feelings for God or illustrate things God has done or made. Tape your stained-glass worship scenes to a large window or show the pictures one by one using an overhead projector. Finish by looking at the pictures as you sing the worship song.

God, we want to worship you
For who you are and what you do.
You are strong and powerful,
Ever-present, wonderful.
We worship you, God.
We worship you, God.
We worship you, God
To show our love for you.

Consider presenting a "slide show" to another class or the adult congregation by showing kids' scenes on an overhead projector. Let kids remind others that we worship God for who he is and for what he does. Then close with the worship song kids just learned. If you want, write the words to the song on a transparency and invite everyone to sing along!

WELCOME, FRIENDS
Welcoming others to worship
1 Peter 5:14

Whatcha Need: You'll need colorful markers, sequins or tiny plastic jewels, craft glue, and self-adhesive name tags. You'll also want to have a table in the church entry with markers and the decorated name tags so kids can sign church attendees' names upon their arrival to the worship service.

Whatcha Do: Plan on this service-oriented project a week or two before you plan to use the name tags. Hand each child a sheet of self-adhesive name tags and invite kids to decorate the edges of the name tags using colorful markers and sequins or small plastic jewels. On the appointed day, set out the blank name tags and markers and have kids write the names of people entering church on the tags. Have people affix their special name tags to their collars. Be sure to have kids warmly welcome people to worship with a special greeting, hug, or handshake. You may wish to ask the pastor to give everyone a special welcome also. Challenge churchgoers to meet and greet five other people by name either before or after the service. Remind everyone that worship is a corporate expression of our love for God and becomes even more joyous when we actively share worship with one another.

THE WORSHIP WALL
Thanking God for what he does
Hebrews 12:28

Whatcha Need: You'll need duct tape, tempera paints or Bingo daubers in a variety of colors, glitter glue, a hole punch, permanent markers, scissors, a white plastic shower-curtain liner, and ribbon or yarn.

Whatcha Do: Choose a place in your classroom or in a church hall where passersby can interact with your wonderful worship wall. Have kids use colorful Bingo daubers or tempera paints to paint the following title across the top of a plastic shower-curtain liner: "Join Us In Worshiping the LORD!" While the title line dries, paint or decorate with glitter glue a 3-inch-wide border around the shower curtain's other three sides. After the paints and glitter glue are dry, punch a hole in the top two corners of the shower curtain and a hole along each side edge about halfway to the bottom of the liner. Cut four 3-foot lengths of ribbon or yarn and tie one end of each length to a permanent marker. Tie the other ends through the holes so that people may use the markers to write on the worship wall. Tape the wall in place in a hallway outside your door or in a place where all church members are encouraged to add their praises, prayers, and words of worship.

Brainstorm things God has done for us that we worship him for, such as how he created beautiful oceans or the forgiveness he gave us through Jesus. Then have each child write one worship praise on the wall using the permanent markers. (Sign your names on the worship wall, if you desire.)

WORSHIP WRAPS
Worshiping in spirit and in truth
John 4:23, 24

Whatcha Need: You'll need a Bible, leather laces, scissors, white and purple pony beads, and fine-tipped black permanent markers.

Whatcha Do: Be sure you have at least six white beads and five purple beads for each person. Cut the leather laces into 10-inch lengths. Invite a volunteer to read aloud John 4:23, 24 and briefly discuss what it means to worship in spirit and in truth and why God desires our worship to be sincere, true, and guided by the Holy Spirit. Then have kids string five purple beads on their leather laces, then six white beads. Use fine-tipped black permanent markers to write the word "spirit" on the white beads, one letter per bead. Write the word "truth" on the purple beads, one letter per bead. Then have kids help each other tie the leather laces around their wrists. Leave a ½-inch end on the ties, then snip off excess leather. If you have older kids, add three more beads (blue or green) and write a J on one bead for "John," a "4:" on one bead to show the chapter reference, and "23" on the third bead to show the verse for John 4:23.

ALTAR LILIES
Worshiping anytime and anyplace
Psalms 29:2; 43:4; 99:5

Whatcha Need: You'll need 1½-inch-wide white wire-edged ribbon and green wire-edged ribbon, green florists' tape, green markers, scissors, and a 12-inch dowel rod for each person.

Whatcha Do: Before class, cut the white and green ribbon into 8-inch lengths. Cut one end of each strip into a point so it looks like the shape of a ski. Cut six white "petals" and six green "leaves" for each person. (Older kids can cut their own ribbons during class.)

Gather kids and invite volunteers to read aloud Psalms 29:2; 43:4; and 99:5. Explain that we can worship God in many places, such as our hearts, our homes, our churches, or even while taking a walk in the woods! Anytime we come before God with a sincere heart of love, honor, and praise for God, we are worshiping him. Tell kids that the altar at church is a special place at the front of the church where we worship. And just as we may give someone flowers for a special place in their home, we like to give God beautiful flowers to place on the altar of his home: our church. Tell kids you will be making lovely altar lilies to place on the altar next week.

For each altar lily, begin by using green markers to color a dowel-rod "stem." Then gather six white-ribbon "petals" and hold them with the pointed tips pointing upwards. Scrunch the bottom halves of the petals to the wooden stem and wrap the petal bottoms to the stem using green florists' tape. Shape the petals by curling them outward and down with your fingers. Take three green leaves and scrunch the bases of the leaves around the florists' tape on the wooden stem. Bend the leaves outward, then wrap them around the stem using florists' tape. Arrange the finished lilies in a lovely vase or bottle and place them on the altar for worship services the following week.

For another lily-making method, have kids trace their hands on white construction paper, then cut out the paper hands. (For each lily, kids must cut five of their paper hand prints.) Attach the bottoms of the paper hands with florists' tape to the dowel rods or green chenille wires. Parents will treasure these special hand lilies for years!

TRAVEL SPOTS

Praying for others
1 Timothy 2:1; Philemon 4; James 5:16

Whatcha Need: You'll need a Bible, pages from (or colored copies of) an old world atlas or local road maps, markers, tacky craft glue, white foam board cut into 4-inch circles, scissors, duct tape, an old file folder or cardboard, and large safety pins.

Whatcha Do: Before class, cut 3-inch cardboard circle patterns for kids to trace and cut around. Be sure the foam board is cut into 4-inch circles. (If you'd rather not use foam board, you can also use poster board, though it will not be as sturdy as foam board.) Ask kids if they've ever asked someone to help a friend or family member. Remind kids that God wants us to ask his help for others as well as for ourselves. Explain that when we pray for others, it is called "intercessory prayer." Invite someone to read aloud James 5:16, then tell kids that God wants us to pray for others each day, whether it is for a friend, family member, or that nations around the world have peace and find God. Point out that we can "travel" to many places to help others when we pray for them.

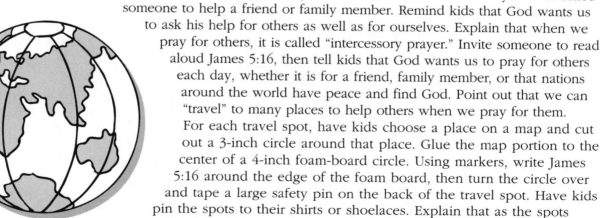

For each travel spot, have kids choose a place on a map and cut out a 3-inch circle around that place. Glue the map portion to the center of a 4-inch foam-board circle. Using markers, write James 5:16 around the edge of the foam board, then turn the circle over and tape a large safety pin on the back of the travel spot. Have kids pin the spots to their shirts or shoelaces. Explain that as the spots travel with them throughout the day, they are reminders to stop and pray for the people in the area on the maps.

GRACE MATS
Worshiping God for his gift of grace
Ephesians 2:8-10

Whatcha Need: You'll need a Bible, a plastic shower-curtain liner (solid colored), permanent markers, glitter glue, and scissors.

Whatcha Do: Cut the plastic shower-curtain liner into 18-by-10-inch rectangles, one per child. (Be sure to use a solid-colored liner such as white, light yellow, or blue.) Ask kids what it means to say "grace" before a meal, then ask them how saying grace is a way to worship God. Explain that grace is undeserved kindness or forgiveness and that God gives us the gift of his grace for which we thank him at meals and through prayers. Invite a volunteer to read aloud Ephesians 2:8-10, then briefly discuss how God's grace saved us from sin and eternal death. Point out that it is at mealtimes when we say grace and thank God for his goodness that we don't deserve but that he lovingly gives us anyway. Hand out the plastic "grace mats" and have kids write Ephesians 2:8 in the centers using permanent markers. Then let kids decorate and embellish their grace mats using colored markers and glitter glue. Finally, demonstrate how to fringe the edges of the mats by making 1-inch cuts all along the sides of the mats or around all four edges. Challenge kids to pray Ephesians 2:8 (or 8-10) at meal-time for the next week as a reminder of God's great grace and why we worship and thank him for his precious gift.

Whatcha Know!

Shower-curtain liners are inexpensive and provide many grace mats. Have kids make a set of grace mats for their families to use at mealtimes. Include different verses about God's grace, forgiveness, or love on each mat. What a worshipful service idea for families!

SWEET SERVICE
Worshiping God by serving others
Deuteronomy 6:5; Galatians 5:13

Whatcha Need: You'll need index cards, scissors, markers, a cookie jar, and a package of cookies.

Whatcha Do: On index cards, write ways for kids to serve God and others during the week. (You may repeat suggestions, but be sure there is at least one card for each person.) Suggestions might include:

- *Make a cheery card for a sick person.*
- *Invite a friend to church.*
- *Visit a neighbor and offer to do a chore.*
- *Read five verses from Psalms each night for a week.*
- *Write a poem to God thanking him for his love.*
- *Tell three friends about Jesus this week.*
- *Pray with a family member this week.*
- *Make a sign for your front door praising God.*

Whatcha Know!

Make photocopies of the serving ideas, then cut them apart. During worship when the collection plate is passed, have kids choose a card and sign it to place in the collection plate as a commitment and a way of giving to God from their hearts during the week.

Place the cards in the cookie jar along with the package of cookies. Have kids take a cookie from the cookie jar as you visit about how sweet it is to serve God as a way to worship him. Remind kids there are many ways to worship God by serving others, but the important thing is to carry through our plans to serve. After kids enjoy their treats, let them reach in the jar again to choose a sweet way to worship God this week. Tell kids they will have time next week to share about their serving experiences.

ROCK OF FAITH

The wonder-working power of faithful prayer
Romans 12:12; 1 Thessalonians 5:17, 18

Whatcha Need: You'll need smooth medium-sized stones, 8-inch fabric squares, rubber bands, scissors, ribbon, a hole punch, and copies of the poem from this activity.

Whatcha Do: Read aloud Romans 12:12 and 1 Thessalonians 5:17, 18 and discuss why faithful prayers and praying every day demonstrate to God our patience and trust in him. Remind kids that God wants us to pray every day and that faithful prayer shows God we enjoy spending time with him. Show kids how to make a fun prayer reminder by placing the smooth stones in the center of the fabric squares (wrong side facing up). Pull the edges of the fabric up around the stones and secure the tops with rubber bands. Punch a hole in the corner of each prayer poem and thread an 8-inch length of ribbon through the hole. Tie the ribbons around the rubber bands.

ROCK-SOLID PRAYERS!

Place this prayer stone on your pillow
Till daylight is no more—
And when you turn your covers back,
It will fall upon the floor.
It's a small yet powerful reminder
To help you kneel and pray,
And speak with words of thanks and love
To your Father every day!

ROCK-SOLID PRAYERS!

Place this prayer stone on your pillow
Till daylight is no more—
And when you turn your covers back,
It will fall upon the floor.
It's a small, yet powerful reminder
To help you kneel and pray;
And speak with words of thanks and love
To your Father every day!

20 PRAYER MODEL
Discovering the parts of prayer
Luke 11:1-4; Colossians 4:2

Whatcha Need: You'll need construction paper, pencils, tape, scissors, glue sticks, markers and crayons, and photocopies of the finger strips from page 108.

Whatcha Do: Make a copy of the finger strips from page 108 for each person. (There are two boxes, so be sure to copy both boxes for each child.) Hand each person a sheet of construction paper and fold the papers in half so that the fold runs down the left side. Let kids work in pairs to position the edges of their left hands along the fold. (Be sure kids' left hands are placed so that the pinky and palm run alongside the fold.) Trace kids' hands from the top of the pinky all the way around to the base of the wrist. (The trace lines should begin and end on the fold.) Keep the papers folded and cut out the hands so they open up like a hand-shaped book. Have each person cut two 4-by-2-inch construction-paper strips. Close the prayer hands and, on one side, tape the strip across the hand running from just below the thumb across to the other side. (Kids will slide their hands in these strips.) Now flip the paper hands over and do the same on the other side. When the strips are attached, open the paper hands. Cut apart the finger-strip boxes and tape or glue them to the fingers as indicated below:

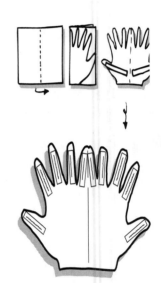

Left thumb: Meet and greet
Left forefinger: Require and desire
Left middle finger: Confession
Left ring finger: Intercession
Left pinky: Thank-you

Right thumb: Dear loving and powerful God,
Right forefinger: Please help me grow closer to you.
Right middle finger: Forgive my hurtful words and selfish things I do.
Right ring finger: Please help me help others to know you, too.
Right pinky: Thank you, dear Father—I love you! Amen.

Have kids slip their hands into the strips and open and close their paper prayer hands. Explain that the words on the left side help us remember what is covered in prayer and that the words on the right fingers give kids an example of a prayer they may pray if they are having trouble thinking of their own. Briefly discuss what each finger of prayer on the left hand means, then let kids find quiet places in the room to pray silently to God using their prayer hands as help and guidance.

DEVOTIONS & OBJECT LESSONS

Bible-bound lessons presented in snappy devotions and object talks to keep kids growing closer to God and their faith!

A Bit of Background

What can grab a child's attention in a second while creating a memory to last a lifetime? Effective object talks, of course! Skillfully presented object talks turn everyday items into constant reminders of God's grace, Christ's love, and the Holy Spirit's empowerment. Kids love snappy devotions built around simple objects, dynamic displays, and surprising stunts. And the best part? Kids remember the messages! Short lessons involving concrete objects help kids visualize meanings and important truths found in God's Word. Jesus knew the value of effective object talks as well. Remember how Jesus taught us about building our lives on solid faith and not on the shifting sands of worldly things? Jesus' students were very aware of sand and how it shifts and is not a stable foundation to build on. By utilizing concrete items and examples during devotions, you're on the way to ensuring understanding and life application in age-appropriate ways for kids. Here are a few tried and true tips about developing and presenting powerful object talks to kids of any age.

✳ **Begin object talks with a surprising fact, feat, or find. For example, gathering kids and giving them a "discover-n-do" challenge such as "How do I get this egg in such a small bottle?" is much more effective than simply saying, "Anything is possible with faith." Grab kids' attention and get them motivated through amazing facts, surprising stunts, or interesting discoveries.**

✳ **Encourage kids to present object talks whenever possible. What's the best way to learn something? Many educational experts say the answer is to teach it! Helping others learn is a powerful way to lock in that learning, and peers helping peers is an exciting way to present object talks. Simply photocopy the message you wish a volunteer to present (along with the object, if possible) and hand it to him the week before class to practice. Kids love presenting messages to their peers—and remember: We all have a lesson to learn and one to share!**

✳ **End object talks with a summary sentence. A short sentence at the close of a devotion helps to refocus the theme, to reinforce the Bible truth, and to clarify the meaning, so be sure to end with summary statements such as "Through Jesus' forgiveness of our sins, we can live nearer to God" or "Serving others is always a way to serve God." Help kids put into simple words the core of the message so it sticks with them like a strong magnet. In other words, summarize to magnetize!**

FAITH FILLED
Lives filled with faith withstand troubles
Psalm 62:6, 7; Mark 4:40

Whatcha Need: You'll need a Bible, two plastic 2-liter bottles (with tops), and water.

Whatcha Do: Fill one bottle with water to the top and replace the cap securely. (The bottle should be so full that it appears empty.) Place the cap on the empty bottle. Before the object talk, set both bottles on the floor on their sides. (Don't let kids see that one bottle has water in it.) Tell kids that you have two plastic bottles that look the same but that have a big difference. Point to the empty bottle and explain that this bottle represents a life not filled with faith and love for God. Hold your foot over the bottle and tell kids that troubles often loom over us and threaten to crush us. Ask kids what they think might happen if troubles descend on a life not filled with faith. Then step on the bottle to crush it. Point out that lives without God and faith are easily destroyed by troubles, sin, worries, and other difficulties.

Now hold your foot over the other bottle. Tell kids this bottle represents a life filled with faith and love for God. Ask kids what might happen to a faith-filled life when we have troubles. Step on the bottle a few times to show kids that lives filled with faith cannot be easily crushed or destroyed. Invite a volunteer to read aloud Psalm 62:6, 7 and Mark 4:40. Then discuss why having faith keeps us strong and not afraid. Point out that, although they couldn't see anything in this bottle, it was filled. Likewise, faith itself cannot be seen, but what faith produces can easily be seen in our strength, courage, self-control, and peace of mind. We don't need to worry or be afraid of anything when we have lives filled with faith. End with a prayer asking God to help you have more faith in him to keep you strong and fearless.

SURROUNDED
God saves us from sin and evil
Job 1:10; 2 Timothy 4:18

Whatcha Need: You'll need a Bible, two toilet-tissue tubes, markers, newspapers, and a medium-sized box.

Whatcha Do: Before the object lesson, color the tissue tubes to look like people. Be sure you have a sheet of newspaper for each person. In addition, make sure that the box is tall and wide enough to hide the tissue-tube people when it's turned upside-down over them. Place the tissue-tube people on the floor and have kids stand in a large circle around them. Hand each person a sheet of newspaper. Have kids tear their papers in half and each make two paper wads. Explain that the tissue-tube people represent people who don't know God or embrace his power and protection against evil and sin. Tell kids that the paper wads represent evil and sin in the world and how it tries to bowl us over every day. Have kids toss the paper wads at the tissue-tube people to try to knock them over. When the paper people are bowled over, ask kids to tell how sin, evil, and temptations can knock over people who don't know God in their lives. Then pick up the box and tell kids it represents the protective power of God to surround and save us from sin and evil. Set the paper people upright, then place the box upside-down over them. Have kids retrieve the paper wads and try again to knock over the people. (Of course, they won't be able to!) Then ask kids how God's power and love surrounds and saves us from sin, evil, and other destructive temptations. Read aloud Job 1:10 and 2 Timothy 4:18.

Be sure to lead kids to understand that God's gift of Jesus has saved us from eternal sin and death. End by tossing the paper wads in a waste basket as you say, "God's power saves us!"

3. FRIENDLY STEPS

Helping one another resist temptations
1 Corinthians 10:13; Galatians 6:1, 2

Whatcha Need: You'll need a Bible, fifteen paper plates, red construction paper, scissors, markers, and tape.

Whatcha Do: Before message time, number the paper plates from 1 to 15. Then tape paper plates around the floor and about 3 feet apart (just far enough so kids will really need to hop from plate to plate). Cut the red construction paper into 3-inch squares, two squares per person. Hand each player two red squares and gather kids by the plate with the number 1. Have kids get with partners (you may have a trio if needed). Explain that in this game the floor represents evil temptations such as stealing, lying, and cheating and that the paper plates represent safe areas. Tell kids that the object of the game is for partners to help one another travel around the room on the paper plates without falling into temptations. If a partner falls or needs a helping hand to step on the floor, the other partner may use a red square to help. (Red squares can be stepped on or used to pull someone from temptation.) When partners reach plate 15, they can hop off and give each other high fives for their friendly help.

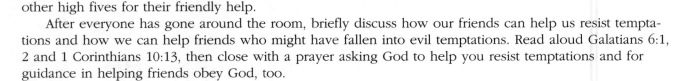

After everyone has gone around the room, briefly discuss how our friends can help us resist temptations and how we can help friends who might have fallen into evil temptations. Read aloud Galatians 6:1, 2 and 1 Corinthians 10:13, then close with a prayer asking God to help you resist temptations and for guidance in helping friends obey God, too.

4. WORKING AS ONE

Everyone is important in Christ's body
Romans 12:4-8; 1 Corinthians 12:12-14

Whatcha Need: You'll need a Bible, ballpoint pens (the kinds with retractable points), and white copy paper.

Whatcha Do: Before this object talk, remove the inner springs from the pens, then reassemble them. The pens should look just fine but will not work properly. Keep the springs nearby but out of sight of kids. Distribute paper and pens to the kids and have them find a place in the room where they can write comfortably. Ask kids to think for a moment before they write down what they feel is the most important part of a pen. Is it the handle so you can hold the pen? Perhaps it's the ink that carries our messages onto paper. Or is it the point with which we write? Have kids write or draw what the most important part on a pen is. (Of course, they won't be able to do so very easily, if at all!) After a few moments of trying to write, ask kids what they think is wrong. Then tell them that their pens are missing an important part and that because of this the pens cannot work well. Remind kids that each part of a pen is equally important to its working well and that it's the same with members of a church or Christian community. Each person is important and plays a role in working for Jesus. Read aloud 1 Corinthians 12:12-14 and

Romans 12:4-8 and briefly discuss why each person is important in working as one for the Lord. Then close by having kids list on their papers the important things they can do to serve Jesus in his church or to serve others outside the church.

HEAVENLY ADDITION

When we're gathered, Jesus is among us
Matthew 18:20

Whatcha Need: You'll need a Bible, index cards, and markers.

Whatcha Do: Before this message, use index cards and markers to make a set of twenty addition flash cards. (If your class is very large, make 6-by-10-inch poster-board cards instead of index cards.) Use simple addition problems and write the answers on the backs of the cards. Make three cards for "1 + 1" but list the answer on the back of each card as "3." One another card, write: "For where two or three

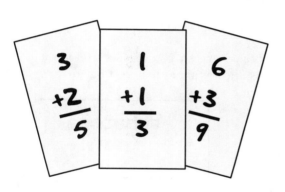

come together in my name, there am I with them" (Matthew 18:20). Shuffle the flash cards, making sure the last card is the one with the verse written on it. Ask kids how good they think they are at addition, then flash the cards one at a time as kids shout out the answers. When you come upon the first "1 + 1" card and kids shout out the answer of "2," turn over the card and show kids the answer is "3." Then look a bit puzzled and say, "Strange. I wonder what that could mean?" and continue on with the rest of the cards. Each time you come to a "1 + 1" card, ask kids if they can think of why the answer might be three instead of two, then continue on through the rest of the cards until you reach the card with the verse on it. Act a bit surprised, then smile and tell kids you have a clue as to why one plus one could equal three. Show the card and have kids look up and read the verse aloud. Briefly discuss what Jesus meant when he said if we're gathered in his name he will be with us. Remind kids that Jesus is always with us but that he especially likes it when we gather in his name. End with a prayer thanking Jesus for being present among us when friends and families gather in his name.

GIVE THE GIFT

When we share God's love, we receive love
Luke 6:38

Whatcha Need: You'll need a Bible and a sack of chocolate candy kisses or candy hearts.

Whatcha Do: Be sure you start with a chocolate candy kiss (or three candy hearts) for each person. Gather kids in a circle and hand each person a candy kiss or three candy hearts. Point out that you are freely giving away the candies, that kids do not have to earn them or pay for them. Then tell kids that they do have a choice to make: They can either keep their candy to eat or may give it away to someone else. Challenge kids to think about their choices, then allow one minute for kids to act on their decisions.

After a minute is up, ask for a show of hands of who decided to keep their candy and who chose to give it away. Ask kids why they made the choices they made. Then tell kids that the candy kisses represent God's love and how he freely gives us this gift. Remind kids that Jesus freely gave his life to forgive our sins, and explain that when we share God's love and Christ's forgiveness we receive even more in return! Read aloud Luke 6:38. Ask for kids who gave away their candies to raise their hands again, then hand each two candy kisses in return. Challenge kids to share God's love during the week and watch how it returns to them in abundance.

   Encourage older kids to share this object talk with children in another class. Let them present the kisses to other kids, then tell about sharing God's love and receiving even more love, forgiveness, grace, and mercy from him.

HEART CONTROL

Softened hearts are open to God
Exodus 9:34; Proverbs 28:14; Romans 7:5, 6

Whatcha Need: You'll need a Bible, a pencil, a raw egg, and a hard-boiled egg.

Whatcha Do: Using a pencil, make a small dot on the hard-boiled egg so you can secretly tell it apart from the raw egg. (Remember which egg is which!) Gather kids and tell them that you have two eggs that look very much the same but that actually have an important difference. Invite two volunteers to spin the eggs on their larger tips. (The raw egg will fall over and be unable to spin, while the hard-boiled egg should spin on its larger point quite easily!) Ask other kids to try spinning the egg until everyone has had a turn on one of the eggs. Hold up the hard-boiled egg and explain that when we have hard, cold, unfeeling hearts we can be easily spun around and controlled through sin (spin the hard-boiled egg.) but that when our hearts are softened through our love for God we cannot be spun around and controlled by earthly things or sin. When our hearts are softened and open to God, we're not easily controlled. Remind kids how Pharaoh's heart was hard as he tried to hurt God's people. Read aloud Exodus 9:34; Proverbs 28:14; and Romans 7:5, 6. Discuss how people harden their hearts and how they can soften them to be open to God. Then offer a prayer asking God to keep your hearts open to him so you won't be controlled by the sinful nature. Challenge kids to present this object at home for their families and friends.

> ## Whatcha Know!
>
> Drop the raw egg in a glass of water and see if you can make it float by stirring in salt. (Use about a half cup of salt.) As the eggs floats, remind kids that when we stir the love and forgiveness of Jesus into our hearts he lightens our worries and burdens!

THE BRIDGE

Jesus is our bridge to heaven
John 14:6

Whatcha Need: You'll need a Bible, a paper plate, a blue marker, powdered gelatin (unflavored), a piece of wool or other static-prone fabric, and an inflated balloon.

Whatcha Do: Before class, rub the balloon on a piece of wool to form a static charge. Make swirls on a paper plate using a blue marker or crayon, then write the following words on the plate: lies, evil, cheating, hurts, and temptation. Write the word "heaven" on the inflated balloon. (You may want to use a permanent marker so the letters don't smudge.) Set the plate on a table and pour the powdered gelatin in the center of the plate. As you rub the balloon on a piece of wool, ask kids what a bridge is good for and how it works. Point out how wonderful and important a bridge is when we need to go someplace and must cross dangerous waters. Then ask kids how life is like a dangerous pool of water. (Point to the words on the paper plate.) Remind kids that temptation, wicked people, hurtful words and actions, and lies are swirling in the dangerous waters of life. Tell kids the gelatin crystals on the plate symbolize us and that the balloon represents heaven, where we want to live someday. Rub the balloon on the wool several more times as you tell kids that we need a special bridge to cross. Then hold the static-charged side of the balloon a few inches over the powdered gelatin. (The gelatin will fly off of the plate and stick to the balloon!) Ask kids if they know who is the special bridge to God and heaven. Invite a volunteer to read aloud John 14:6, then briefly discuss how Jesus forms a bridge between the world and our Father in heaven and how we can choose to make Jesus the "way" in our lives. Point out how the static's power allowed the crystals to rise and how Jesus' power to love and forgive our sins allows us to have eternal life in heaven. Close with a prayer thanking Jesus for providing a bridge to our heavenly Father.

Kids may enjoy making their own balloons and paper plates so they can present this object talk at home for their families and friends. (Flavored gelatin will work but requires a bit longer to rub the balloon.)

CHOICE MATTERS
God gives us free choice to use wisely
Joshua 24:15; Proverbs 16:16

Whatcha Need: You'll need a Bible, masking tape, pennies (one for every two kids), paper plates, and markers.

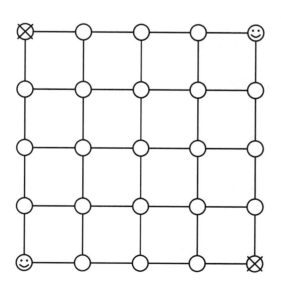

Whatcha Do: Before message time, place a masking tape grid on the floor according to the diagram. Tape paper plates at the intersecting lines, then draw Xs on two of the plates (at opposite corners of the grid) and two happy faces on the plates at the other corners. Have kids get with partners and hand each pair a penny to flip. Tell partners to choose a paper plate to stand on but not on a plate with a happy face or an X. Explain that this is a game of choices and that the object is to end the game on a paper plate with a happy face, which symbolizes obedience to God. Tell kids the paper plates with Xs represent disobeying God. Explain that when you say "flip," partners flip their coins and move one plate to the right or left with heads being right and tails being left. If partners come to the end of a row and cannot move left (or right), they can choose whether to move one plate ahead or behind where they are standing. If someone lands on a happy face plate or a plate with an X, she is to stay where she is (standing beside the plate so others can land there, too). Point out that players may be forced to move to a happy face or X and have to stop there. Tell kids there will be ten flips of the coins to move and make choices.

At the end of ten flips, see which partners have made it to the goal of the happy faces or if anyone was caught on a plate with an X. Then ask kids to sit in place and briefly discuss how this game is like the choices we make in life that draw us closer to God or send us further away from him. Ask what influence partners had on choices and how other people influence our choices about God in real life. Invite volunteers to read aloud Joshua 24:15b and Proverbs 16:16, then discuss why it's important to choose serving and following God over disobeying him. Point out that many times people flip coins to make decisions but that when we know, love, and follow God we seek *him* as the answer to our choices! Play the game once more, then close with a prayer asking God to help you make wise choices that draw you closer to him.

LET GO, THEN LET GOD!
God frees us from sin and offers forgiveness
Acts 3:19, 20; Romans 8:2

Whatcha Need: You'll need a Bible, a bag of jelly beans, and a large plastic or glass jar. (The mouth of the jar needs to be large enough to insert your hand but tight enough so that your fist cannot be removed without first opening your hand.)

Whatcha Do: Place the jelly beans in the jar and set the jar on a table. Gather kids around and greedily tell them you have goodies in a jar and can't wait to try one. Reach in the jar and grab a handful of jelly beans in your fist, then try to remove your hand. When you find that it's stuck, be a bit expressive and tell kids you have a big problem: Your hand is stuck and you're trapped. (Ham it up a bit to show how stuck your hand is!) Tell kids you're being held captive by the jar and there seems to be no escape! Ask what you should do and, when someone suggests letting go of the jelly beans, act surprised. Tell kids you hadn't thought of that, then let go of the beans and open your hand to let it slide free of the jar. When your hand is removed, act relieved and tell kids you're so happy to be free at last! Explain that this is like being held captive by sin, that when we hold on to things God tells us are wrong we become enslaved to those things and aren't free in our hearts and lives. Point out that sometimes we do things we know are wrong. We want God to forgive us but don't want to turn loose of the sin. As long as we hold on to sin, we're held captive and can't receive God's forgiveness. Ask kids to tell how we can be free through Jesus' forgiveness and what being free from sin means. Read aloud Acts 3:19, 20 and Romans 8:2, then briefly discuss how our lives change when we no longer are held captive by sin. Remind kids that when we let go of the negatives in our lives and turn to Jesus he sets us free from sin and death. Close by giving everyone a jelly bean or two as sweet reminders to "let go and let God" work in their lives.

PRAYER CUPS
The purpose of prayer in our lives
Philippians 4:6, 7; James 5:15, 16

Whatcha Need: You'll need a Bible, 8-inch squares of white copy paper or stiff wrapping paper, colorful markers, and a pitcher of water.

Whatcha Do: Gather kids and ask them what they do when they're thirsty. Then ask:

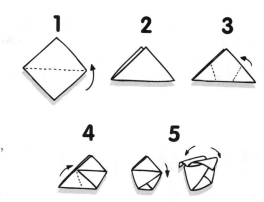

- Does drinking warm milk quench your thirst? Why not?
- Does eating peanut butter quench your thirst? Explain.

Encourage kids to tell why taking a drink of water helps quench their thirst better than any other drink or food. Remind kids that water refreshes us when we're thirsty in the same way that prayers refresh our hearts when we have everyday troubles, worries, and needs. Explain that nothing refreshes us the way talking to God does! Read aloud Philippians 4:6, 7 and James 5:15, 16. Then demonstrate how to fold a drinking cup using squares of paper. Have kids follow along in the folding directions. When the cups are finished, have kids write 1 Thessalonians 5:17 on their cups to remind them that prayer is a wonderful and refreshing way to worship God! When the verses are written and the cups decorated using markers, let kids take a drink from their cups, then share a prayer thanking God for the gift of prayer.

INSIDE 'N OUT
A pure heart is important
1 Samuel 16:7; Psalm 51:10; Matthew 5:8

Whatcha Need: You'll need a Bible, a fine-tipped permanent marker, a slip of paper, a straight pin, and three large balloons in the following colors: one white and two orange.

Whatcha Do: Prior to this object lesson, write the following words on a slip of paper: "unkind words," "lying," "cheating," disobeying God," and "selfishness." Fold the paper and stuff it inside one of the orange balloons. Inflate and tie the orange balloon. Inflate the white balloon (but do not tie it yet) and draw a heart on the balloon. Write the following words inside the heart: "love," "patience," "kindness," "forgiveness," and "obedience." Let the air out of the white balloon. Slide the white balloon inside the other orange balloon and hold both ends of the balloons as you inflate the inner white balloon. As the white balloon expands, it will expand the orange balloon as well. Pull the white end out a bit, then tie a knot in the white balloon. Continue blowing up the orange balloon so it is a bit larger than the inside balloon. Tie the white knot and orange end together. (You should now have a balloon within a balloon and one knot to keep them inflated.) During the message, you'll carefully pop the outer orange balloon by pricking it with a pin near the top (being careful not to pop the white balloon, too).

Gather kids and show them the balloons. Explain that the balloons look pretty much the same on the outside but that they're different on the inside. Pop the orange balloon holding the slip of paper and have someone read the words aloud. Tell kids that this balloon represents people who look fine on the outside but who have mean and hurtful hearts on the inside. Then pop the other orange balloon to reveal the white balloon on the inside. Invite a volunteer to read aloud the words on the heart shape. Explain that God wants us to be as good

---

Whatcha Know!

If you have extra balloons, kids will enjoy preparing the balloons for this object talk to take home and share with their families and friends!

on the inside as we appear on the outside. Tell kids that when we know, love, and follow the Lord our hearts become pure and sweet. Point out that God knows what's inside our hearts and that we want him to see goodness, kindness, and love. Read aloud 1 Samuel 16:7; Psalm 51:10; and Matthew 5:8. Close with a prayer asking God to help your hearts be pure and to let your kindness on the inside shine through to the outside for everyone to see.

MARK THE PATH
God helps us find the right way to go
Psalm 25:4; Luke 1:78, 79; John 16:13

Whatcha Need: You'll need a Bible, clear self-adhesive paper, glitter or small confetti hearts, fine-tipped permanent markers (black), and scissors.

Whatcha Do: Gather kids and ask what helps them find their way when they become lost or confused with what direction to take. Then remind kids that God always helps us find our way and guides us in truth. Read Psalm 25:4; Luke 1:78, 79; and John 16:13. Briefly discuss how God guides us and why it's important to follow and obey his leading. Then tell kids that when we sing songs from hymnals or look up verses in the Bible, it's sometimes helpful to have a special marker to help us find our way to a certain song or passage. Explain that you'll be making special path markers to place in the church's Bibles or hymnals so church members can find their way to certain songs and verses during the church service. Show kids how to cut a 14-inch length of clear self-adhesive paper and place it carefully on the table, sticky side up. Sprinkle glitter or confetti down the center of one half of the tape, then carefully fold the tape in half to trap the glitter. Snip off any uneven corners. Then use permanent black markers to write reminders of God's guidance on the markers such as, "The Bible leads to God," "God helps us find our way," "Jesus is the way, the truth, and the life," or "God guides us." Place the path markers in Bibles or hymnals or give them to church members as special keepsakes and reminders of God's gracious guidance in our lives.

> ## Whatcha Know!
>
> Try one of these colorful variations to make your path markers even more special.
> • Punch a hole at one end of each marker and attach a colorful tassel or ribbon.
> • Make three markers and tie them together with a 4-inch ribbon to make a 3-in-1 marker and great reminder and object lesson on the Trinity.

OBEY TODAY
Obeying God gives him honor
Matthew 3:16, 17; 1 John 5:3

Whatcha Need: You'll need a Bible, white construction paper, scissors, tape, colorful markers, and a variety of bright ribbon (solid-colored or in stripes and patterns).

Whatcha Do: Before this object talk, cut ribbon into 8-inch lengths. Use a festive variety of ribbon such as bright neon or solid colors and stripes, stars, or other lively patterns. You may wish to cut out several dove patterns from old file folders to let kids trace around. Invite volunteers to read aloud 1 John 5:3, then remind kids that one of the best ways to express our love and honor for God is to obey him. Briefly discuss ways to obey God, such as reading the Bible, helping others, being encouraging, and forgiving one another. Then lead kids to understand why obedience is crucial to giving God our love. Remind kids that Jesus obeyed God when he went to the Jordan River to be baptized and that as the dove descended to Jesus God spoke his pleasure at Jesus' obedience. Read aloud Matthew 3:16, 17. Distribute the white paper and show kids how to fold their papers in half and draw or trace a simple dove shape on their papers. (Be sure the ends of the tails are against the fold.) Cut out the doves so they fold open, then write the words to 1 John 5:3 on the insides of the folded doves. List ways to obey God on the ribbons. Suggestions might include through prayer, reading the Bible, helping others, saying kind words, or sharing with someone. Tape the ribbon streamers to the backs of the doves, then challenge kids to worship God by doing the things on their ribbons during the coming week.

GONE FOREVER!

Jesus replaces our sins with forgiveness
Psalm 103:2, 3; Romans 4:7; Colossians 2:13, 14

Whatcha Need: You'll need a Bible, a men's handkerchief, white paper, a pen, scissors, a white glue stick, and a nickel.

Whatcha Do: Try this neat object talk before class to make your presentation smooth. Trace two circles on white paper, using a nickel as your pattern. Write the word "sin" on one circle and the word "forgiveness" on the other. Place a tiny bit of glue from a white glue stick on one corner of the handkerchief and stick the "forgiveness" circle face down to the glue. Place a tiny bit of glue from the glue stick over the word "sin" on the other circle and place that circle right-side up on a table. Spread the handkerchief on the table with the "forgiveness" circle under your left thumb at all times. At the appropriate time in the message, you will place the "sin" circle right-side up in the center of the handkerchief. Fold the corners in to the middle, starting with corner beside the "forgiveness" circle. Push down a bit on the "sin" circle so the glue makes the circle stick to the handkerchief. At the correct time, quickly open the handkerchief as you remove the forgiveness circle under your left thumb. Toss the handkerchief aside (with the "sin" circle still stuck to the corner) and show kids how sin has turned to forgiveness through Jesus!

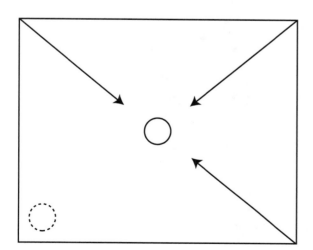

Gather kids around a table and have your handkerchief in hand with the "forgiveness" circle in place under your left thumb. Remind kids that the Bible tells us we all have sinned and have fallen short of God's glory—that we all need Jesus' forgiveness to be close to God and have eternal life. Spread the handkerchief out on the table (keep the circle under your thumb) and place the "sin" circle in the center of the handkerchief. Remind kids that when Jesus gave his life for us on the cross he covered our sins with his love and shed blood. (Place the corners of the handkerchief over the center circle and gently push to make it stick.) Ask kids why they think Jesus willingly covered our sins. Then tell kids that Jesus loved us so greatly that he took on our sins and changed them from sin to forgiveness! Quickly open up the handkerchief as you remove the "forgiveness" circle. Toss aside the handkerchief and let kids read the circle. Read aloud Psalm 103:2, 3; Colossians 2:13, 14; Romans 4:7; and Ephesians 1:7, 8. Then offer a prayer thanking Jesus for removing our sins and replacing them with his loving forgiveness.

 # SWEET WISDOM

God's Word is sweet and true
Psalm 119:103; Proverbs 2:6; 23:23

Whatcha Need: You'll need a Bible, 1-by-2-inch slips of copy paper, a fortune cookie, markers or pens, a bowl of melted chocolate coating (the kind that hardens into a shell-like coating), a plastic spoon, waxed paper, and curled potato chips (kettle-cooked chips work well).

Whatcha Do: Hold up the fortune cookie and ask kids what you're holding. Ask kids if they think a fortune cookie really holds wisdom or truth and to explain their answers. Remind kids that all truth comes from God and discuss what things God's truth does for us, such as teaches us, guides and helps us obey God, and leads us to live as God desires. Invite volunteers to read aloud Psalm 119:103 and Proverbs 2:6 and 23:23. Ask what it would be like if there was no wisdom or truth from God. Remind kids that God desires us to seek his wisdom and to trust in his Word, which is truth. Form eight small groups and hand out slips of paper and markers or pens. Assign each group one of the following verses about wisdom found in Proverbs and have them write the verse on their slips of paper: 2:6; 2:10; 2:12; 3:13; 4:5; 4:6; 4:7; 4:11. (If your class is small, form four groups and assign each group two verses to read and copy down.) Fold the papers in half and slide them into the curl of a folded potato chip. Dip the edges of the chips into melted chocolate and place the chips on waxed paper to allow the chocolate to harden. As you enjoy nibbling the chips, be sure to read and discuss each wise verse as you discover it.

NO LEAKS!

God stops the hurts that drain us
Job 5:18; Psalm 147:3

Whatcha Need: You'll need a Bible, two plastic bottles with tops, water, and a push pin.

Whatcha Do: Before this object lesson, use one of the bottles to try out this nifty demonstration. Fill one of the plastic bottles full of water and replace the top securely. Poke a push pin into the bottle about 2 inches from the base. Carefully remove the pin and wipe away the drops of water. The leak should amazingly stop! (But if you open the bottle top, the leak will spurt forth.) Prepare the other bottle but do not poke the pin in until message time.

Gather kids and hold up the bottle of water. Explain that the bottle represents us and the love we have inside. Ask kids what things cause us to be hurt or saddened so that it feels as if our love is slipping away. Suggestions might include friends lying, someone who cheats us, family members fighting, or even school worries. Poke the pin into the bottle as you remind kids that hurts, pain, frustrations, and worries are all things that happen in all our lives. Then as you slowly pull the pin away from the bottle, tell kids that just when it seems like hurts and pains should cause us to leak away love, God wipes away our teas (wipe the droplets from the bottle) and binds our hurts to stop the leaks. When we rely on God for help and comfort, God keeps us filled with love. Replace the pin and set the bottle aside. Read aloud Job 5:18 and Psalm 147:3. Then close with a prayer asking God to heal your hurts and to keep you filled with love.

JOY IS THE WORD!

Joy is found in the Lord
Psalms 47:1; 81:1; 98:4; 100:2

Whatcha Need: You'll need Bibles, two paper plates, markers, and tape.

Whatcha Do: Before this object lesson, draw a simple smiley face on one paper plate and a wide-open smiley face on the second plate. Tape the faces at opposite ends of the room where kids can see them. Gather kids in the center of the room and ask them what the difference between the two faces is. Lead kids to see that one smile is bigger than the other. This face represents the joy we feel in God, while the other face shows happiness we feel at earthly things such as ice cream or a favorite toy that makes us happy. Explain the difference between "everyday happy" and true joy in the Lord. Then call out the following and have kids run to stand by the face they think best fits the situation.

- **a favorite television show** (happy)
- **answered prayers** (joy)
- **Jesus taking away worries** (joy)
- **a sunny day** (happy)
- **worshiping God** (joy)
- **passing a spelling test** (happy)
- **being saved by God's grace** (joy)
- **being forgiven by Jesus** (joy)

After playing, invite volunteers to read aloud the following "joy" verses from Psalms: 47:1; 81:1; 98:4; and 100:2. Then close by offering a prayer thanking God for the joy we feel from his love, grace, forgiveness, salvation, and help.

KNOCK-KNOCK

Jesus answers when we seek him
Matthew 7:7; Luke 11:9; John 14:13

Whatcha Need: You'll need a Bible and a door knocker. If you plan on doing the accompanying craft, you'll also need 8-inch plywood squares, a stapler, scissors, paint pens, picture hangers (and hammers, if you need them), ¼-inch-wide ribbon, and large wooden beads.

Whatcha Do: Hold up the door knocker and ask kids to tell what the item is and how it works. Then invite kids to tell about times they might have gone to someone's house and found no one at home. Encourage kids to share how it felt to look for someone and not find them. Tell kids that Jesus made us a special promise, that if we knocked, his door would be open and he would always answer us. Read aloud Matthew 7:7; Luke 11:9; and John 14:13. Then ask kids how Jesus' promise is a demonstration of his love for us. Point out that we never have to worry if Jesus is home or if he will answer when we call to him; he promises to answer us and help at any time and at any place! Read Matthew 7:7 once more, then have kids take turns knocking with the door knocker and repeating the verse.

If there's time, kids will enjoy making their own special door knockers. Attach hangers to the backs of the wooden squares using hammers and the nails provided with the picture hangers, then flip the squares over. Cut 6-inch lengths of ribbon (one or two lengths per person) and staple them to the center tops of the door knockers. Tie large wooden beads to the ends of the ribbons (or slide the beads on the ribbons, then knot the ribbon ends so the beads won't slip off). Snip off any excess ribbon. Finally, use paint pens to decorate the edges of the squares. When the door knockers are dry, show kids how to rap on the wooden squares using the beads.

MORE SUPER SEASONALS

Holiday gifts, seasonal snacks, and bushels of fun help kids celebrate the seasons in style!

A Bit of Background

"For I know the plans I have for you," declares the LORD, "plans to prosper you and not to harm you, plans to give you hope and a future." **Jeremiah 29:11**

There is a time for everything, and a season for every activity under heaven. **Ecclesiastes 3:1**

Perhaps the two verses that best attest a child's spirit of expectancy and desire for stability are Jeremiah 29:11 and Ecclesiastes 3:1. What child doesn't spend the year anticipating Christmas, the first buds of spring, or her birthday? And as surely as school starts every fall, those holidays and seasons will arrive. Why? God has planned it so! It's through the stability of the seasons that God teaches us about trust and assurance, and it's through holidays that we experience what joy and celebration are all about. When God promises us a future and a hope, kids understand more of what this means by knowing the assurance of the hope of spring and the promise of warm days and cool nights. For if God has planned so lovingly for our seasons, how much more he has promised for the glory of our futures with him!

Seasons and their accompanying holidays are one of God's most beautiful and useful gifts to us. And seasonal delights are guaranteed to fill kids with wonder, awe, and merry excitement. Make the most of this natural motivation by offering loads of holiday crafts, seasonal snacks, and dynamic displays throughout the year. The crafts and snacks included in this section of *More 200+ Activities for Children's Ministry* are unique projects that will have your kids smiling proudly. Here are a few quick hints to add more celebration to the seasons.

* **Cover bulletin boards, doors, or walls with seasonal or holiday gift wrap. Large rolls make covering your areas a snap, and the festive patterns lend instant ambiance to your room!**

* **Don't be as predictable as the seasons—offer a wintry craft during the hot summer or try making Valentines during the fall using leaves to form heart shapes.**

* **Make two life-sized kids from foam board or poster board and invite kids to dress them according to the season or holiday using paper clothes creations.**

* **Bring in a potted evergreen tree (real or artificial) and make monthly ornaments to hang on the tree. Glittery leaves are great in the fall, Christmas balls or snowflakes work well for winter, flowers fill the spring, and swirly suns or stars look super in summer!**

SQUIRREL COBS

Help our furry friends prepare for winter.

Whatcha Need: You'll need dried cobs of corn, plastic knives, peanut butter, birdseed or sunflower seeds (unsalted), shower-curtain hooks, string or twine, scissors, paper lunch sacks, and aluminum foil.

Whatcha Do: Pour birdseed or unsalted sunflower seeds into a paper lunch sack. Spread peanut butter over half a cob of corn, then shake the corn cob in the sack of seeds. Remove the corn and attach a shower-curtain hook (the kind that closes much like a safety pin) around the middle of the cob. Cut a 10-inch length of string or twine and tie both ends of the string to the shower-curtain hook to make a long loop for hanging in a tree or on a fence. As you work, have kids tell how squirrels and other wildlife prepare for the winter. Then remind kids how God helps us prepare for the future as well. Encourage kids to tell how God helps us be prepared for the future. When the squirrel cobs are finished, wrap them in aluminum foil for kids to carry home and hang up.

Here are other harvest-treats that furry, fuzzy, or feathery friends will enjoy!
- Spread pine cones with peanut butter, then roll in thistle seeds for small wrens and cardinals to eat.
- Gather large, dead or fallen tree branches and let each person make a holiday harvest tree by hanging goodies on the branches. Hang bits of wool, crepe paper, and dried grass or straw for animal homes. Hang seed-covered treats on the braches (use peanut-butter "mortar" for seeds to stick to), including soda crackers, tortillas, apple halves, and unsalted peanuts in the shell.

GIGGLE-GAGGLE GEESE

Here's a clever harvest centerpiece kids will love!

Whatcha Need: You'll need scissors (or an awl), whole cloves, orange and black permanent markers, push pins (four per child), and a crookneck squash for each person. (Choose crookneck squash with a portion of the stems still attached; the stems will form the beaks.)

Whatcha Do: Distribute the crookneck squash and ask kids to tell you what kind of vegetables they are holding. Remind kids that God gives us good food to eat and that harvest time is an especially good time to thank God for the bounty of his blessings. Explain that you'll be making a cute gaggle of geese to grace your tables at this thankful time of year. Help kids push the push pins in the bottom of the squash to help the squash "geese" stand upright. (If you prefer not to use push pins, simply slice a slab of squash from the bottom center of each crookneck squash before class.) Use the pointed end of a pair of scissors (or an awl) to make eye holes on the narrow ends of the squash close to the stem "beaks." Push whole cloves in the holes to make the eyes of the geese. Finally, use permanent markers to color the beaks (stems) of the geese orange. Add any other features you desire, such as feathers, by using a black permanent marker.

Consider photocopying directions for cooking the squash after using the geese as centerpieces for several weeks. Simply remove the push pins and chop the squash into several large pieces. Place the squash on a plate, add a few teaspoons of water, and securely cover the squash with plastic wrap. Microwave on medium-high for fifteen minutes or until the squash can be scooped from its shell using a spoon. Add butter and brown sugar for an extra-fine treat!

HARVEST HOLDERS
These bright candle holders celebrate autumn!

Whatcha Need: You'll need newspapers, tacky craft glue, damp paper towels, paper plates, a bag of birdseed mix or other small seeds and crushed corn kernels, glitter, florist's clay, tea-light candles, and a clean, empty baby-food jar and lid for each person.

Whatcha Do: Cover tables with newspapers and pour birdseed and glitter on paper plates. Invite kids to tell what their favorites parts of autumn are and why. Encourage kids to tell how the fall season is different than the other three seasons and ask them to tell why God planned the autumn as he did. Then show kids how to spread tacky craft glue around the outsides of the baby-food jars (using fingers), and roll the sticky jars in birdseed and glitter. (Wipe fingers clean using damp paper towels.) Stick a nickel-sized piece of florist's clay to the bottom of a tea-light candle, then carefully stick the tea light to the inside bottom of the jar. Tell kids to have an adult light their special candles during dinner as they give thanks to God for the wonders of autumn.

Whatcha Know!

Try mixing popcorn kernels and dried peas and beans in a plastic margarine bowl. Add 1 ounce of white craft glue and stir. Let the mixture sit for 2 minutes, then push a taper candle in the center. Allow the mixture to dry 12 hours, then loosen the edges of the tub. The candle and holder will pop right out!

CORNUCOPIA COUNTDOWN
Count your blessings and the days 'til Thanksgiving.

Whatcha Need: You'll need colored construction paper, scissors, fine-tipped markers, two packages of sticky tack, and a 2-foot square of brown foam board for each person.

Whatcha Do: Have kids brainstorm all the things they're thankful for in these categories: family, friends, church, school, nature, foods, and God. Remind kids that Thanksgiving is a holiday set aside to thank God for the blessings he so richly gives us. Then invite kids to find partners to work with and hand everyone a square of brown foam board. Have kids draw a line across and 3 inches above the bottoms of the squares. Then show kids how to draw a simple cornucopia (horn of plenty) shape above the line on their squares. Tear or cut colored construction paper into simple 3-inch food shapes, such as apples, oranges, potatoes, carrots, lemons, pears, plums, and limes. Make thirty shapes (or as many shapes as there are days before Thanksgiving). Have kids jot down on the food shapes things they're thankful for, such as "my family," "ice cream, " or "when Jesus helps me." Have kids place a tiny glob of sticky tack to the back of each shape and attach the shapes below the line under the cornucopias. Tell

Whatcha Know!

If use 30 shapes on your special advent cornucopia, they can be used year after year (no matter when the holiday falls) to count the number of days until Thanksgiving!

kids to choose a food and place it on the cornucopia each day before Thanksgiving and to have their families read the shape and discuss why this is something wonderful to be thankful for.

TURKEY TREATS

These turkeys will get you a-gobblin'!

Whatcha Need: You'll need a bag of candy corn, raisins, paper towels, and double-stuffed sandwich cookies (two to four cookies per child).

Whatcha Do: Hand each person a paper towel and two double-stuffed sandwich cookies. (Double-stuffed cookies have twice the white filling as regular sandwich cookies—some even have orange filling especially for autumn!) Show kids how to carefully untwist both thick sandwich cookies so the filling stays on one half of each cookie. (Set aside the cookie halves with no filling on them to eat later.) Place one cookie half with filling on a paper towel as the base for your tasty turkey. Stick the other cookie half in the filling of your base. This is the turkey body. Carefully stick the points of five candy corns into the filling on the back of each turkey as "feathers." Finally, stick a raisin in front of the turkey body for the head. After you enjoy your tasty turkey treats, sing the following song to the tune of "Oh, My Darlin'" (author unknown). For more fun, make up actions to go along with the words!

Albuquerque is a turkey,
And he's feathered and he's fine.
Oh, he wobbles, and he gobbles,
And he's absolutely mine!
He's the best pet
That you can get—
Better than a dog or cat.
He's my Albuquerque turkey,
And I'm mighty proud of that!

GIVING TREE

Here's a festive holiday service project to try!

Whatcha Need: You'll need an artificial Christmas tree (donated or purchased, since you'll be giving away the tree), construction paper, scissors, tape, markers, ribbon, twist-tie wires or ornament hangers, and personal hygiene items kids bring in as donations, including new combs, toothbrushes, soaps, brushes, washcloths, bubble bath, toothpaste, and lotions.

Whatcha Do: A week or two before your project, send a note home with kids asking for donations of new personal hygiene items. Have each child agree to bring in one or two items to donate to a local homeless shelter. Explain that you'll be decorating a Christmas tree of love for the shelter and that the donations will be some of your gifts to include.

On project day, set up the artificial Christmas tree and have kids hang their items on the tree. You may need to help kids make loops for hanging items using tape and ribbon, or you can use twist-tie wires or ornament hangers to suspend donations from the tree branches. Invite kids to make construction-paper ornaments to hang on the tree. Write favorite verses on the ornaments or joyous holiday messages about Jesus and his loving forgiveness and salvation. Tie ribbon bows to the branches and add a paper or foil star to the tree top. Finish by joining hands around the tree and singing "Silent Night." Be sure to offer a prayer thanking God for the chance to serve him and others through giving your time, donations, and love.

To extend the learning and the fun, read the delightful story of *The Giving Tree* by Shel Silverstein. Ask kids to compare the ways that Jesus gave everything he had to and for us in the same ways the tree gave all it had to give. Then have kids draw pictures of their own giving trees and list ways they can give to others during and after the holiday season to share Jesus' love.

MANGER WREATH
A wreath reminder of the hay in Jesus' manger.

Whatcha Need: You'll need aluminum foil, plastic spoons or craft sticks, white craft glue, plastic bowls (a bowl for every three kids), shredded wheat-type biscuits, and tiny cinnamon candies or small red beads.

Whatcha Do: Have kids form groups of three and hand each group a bowl and three sheets of aluminum foil (8-inch squares). Let kids scrunch shredded wheat biscuits into the bowls (two biscuits per person). Using a plastic spoon, measure 3 spoonfuls of craft glue into the bowl and stir to mix the cereal and glue. (If the wheat is not coated enough, add a bit more glue; if the wheat is too sticky, scrunch another biscuit into the mixture.) Have kids use the wheat-and-glue mixture to form wreaths on their foil squares. Press small cinnamon candies or red beads around the wreaths for a bit of color. Remind kids how Jesus was laid to rest in a manger of hay the night he was born. As you work to form the wreaths, sing "Away in A Manger." When the wreaths are formed, have kids carry them carefully home (or leave them in the room to dry for several hours). Then peel away the foil and add a string or yarn loop for hanging. Remind kids that these special wreaths are not for eating!

ANGELS ON HIGH
These adorable angels remind us of God's grace.

Whatcha Need: You'll need white craft glue, a bowl, water, paintbrushes, newspapers, white construction paper, pencils, paint pens (or fine-tipped permanent markers), 1½-inch beads, scissors, copies of the angel strips from this activity, macramé cord, and 3-inch clay pots (with holes in the bottoms).

Whatcha Do: Spread newspapers over a table. Thoroughly mix one part white craft glue to three parts water in a plastic bowl. Cut 20-inch lengths of macramé cord, one length per person. Hand each child a clay pot, a large bead, and a length of cord. Show kids how to tie a large knot in one end of the cord. Hold the clay pots upside down and thread the cords up through the inside of the pots and out of the holes in the bottoms. (The knots should keep the pots on the cords.) The pot will make the body of each angel. Then slide a 1½-inch bead on each cord and slide it to rest on the bottom of the pot. Tie a knot close to the bead. (The bead form the angel's head.) Using paint pens or fine-tipped permanent markers, add facial details and hair to the angels' heads. Cut apart the angel strips so each person has a set of six strips. Using paintbrushes dipped in the glue-and-water mixture, affix the strips around the clay pots. (Space the strips all around the pots as desired.) Finally, brush the entire pots with the thin glue, then set the angels aside to dry while you prepare the wings. For each set of wings, have kids trace their hands on white construction paper and cut out the hand shapes. When the angels are dry, simply glue the palms of the paper hands to the backs of the clay pots to form wings. If you'd like, glue a bit of tinsel garland to the angels' heads as halos.

Use the following quotes for the angel strips.

We are, each of us angels with only one wing; and we can only fly by embracing one another. — Luciano De Crescenzo

- -

Make yourself familiar with the angels and behold them frequently in spirit; for without being seen, they are present with you. — St. Francis De Sales

- -

Do not forget to entertain strangers, for by doing so some people have entertained angels without knowing it. — Hebrews 13:2

- -

Angels and ministers of grace defend us. — William Shakespeare

- -

With all my heart I praise you, LORD. In the presence of angels I sing your praises. — Psalm 138:1 (Contemporary English Version)

- -

See, I am sending an angel ahead of you to guard you along the way and to bring you to the place I have prepared. — Exodus 23:20

PROMISE BLOCKS

Versatile blocks hold the promise of the New Year!

Whatcha Know!

If you're unable to use wooden blocks, square cardboard boxes will also work for this activity. Or try having kids make a mobile with suspended pictures or cards that express their plans for the coming year.

Whatcha Need: You'll need 6-inch-square wooden blocks (end cuts from a 6-by-6-inch board will work well), sandpaper squares, scissors, old greeting cards from various holidays or a box of "all occasion" cards, paint pens, glitter glue, and tacky craft glue.

Whatcha Do: Invite kids to tell what holidays we usually celebrate each year, then have them tell about other celebrations we may share in our families, such as birthdays, anniversaries, or family reunions. Remind kids that special occasions give us wonderful promises to look forward to. Point out how this is much like looking forward with excitement and great anticipation to the futures God has promised us. Hand each person a wooden block and square of sandpaper. Show kids how to sand their blocks until all six sides are smooth. Then invite kids to choose six holidays, celebrations, or special events they're looking forward to in the new year and express each on a different side of the block. For example, if a child is turning twelve this year, she may want to paint a decorative numeral "12" on one side. Or another person may want to cut a birthday cake from a card and glue it to one side of the cube to represent family birthdays that will be shared. When the promise blocks are completed, have kids stand and show the sides of their blocks as they tell what each side represents.

 # SNOWMAN SOUP
Tasty treats double as service projects and gifts!

Whatcha Need: You'll need insulated foam cups (disposable), packets of hot-cocoa mix, plastic spoons, permanent markers, scissors, wrapped candy canes or hard stick candy, tape, and copies of the Snowman Soup poem from this activity.

Whatcha Do: Have kids use permanent markers to decorate a foam cup as a snowman. (If you're making these for keepsake-type gifts, use plastic mugs and paint pens.) Then cut out and color copies of the Snowman Soup poems and tape the poems to the cups. Place a packet of hot-cocoa mix, a plastic spoon, and a wrapped candy cane or candy "swizzle stick" in each cup.

How does a shivery snowman
Warm up in the wintry air?
He sips a bit of Snowman Soup
And smiles without a care!
So here's some Snowman Soup for you
Complete with a stirring stick.
Just add hot water and sip it down—
It's sure to warm you quick!

 # FLUFFY TRUFFLES
Make and share these special Valentine's treats!

Whatcha Need: You'll need a large bag of milk-chocolate chips, 6 tablespoons of butter, 3 tablespoons of heavy cream, one packet of hot-cocoa mix, plastic spoons, paper plates, pink and red construction paper, scissors, plastic wrap, mixing bowls and spoons, powdered sugar, and access to a microwave oven and a freezer. (Hint: This recipe makes about twenty-four truffles, so plan accordingly for your class size. You may wish to make extra fluffy truffles to share with families and friends.)

Whatcha Do: Let kids help pour the chocolate chips, butter (chopped into smaller pieces), cream, and hot-cocoa mix in a bowl. Pop the bowl into the microwave and cook on high for ninety seconds until the ingredients are almost melted, then stir the mixture until it's smooth. Cover the bowl with plastic wrap, then place it in the freezer for about half an hour. As you wait, have kids prepare the plates to put their truffles on by cutting pink and red hearts from construction paper to lay on the plates. When the truffle mixture is firm, have kids roll spoonfuls in their clean hands, then roll the truffle balls in powdered sugar.

Older kids might enjoy a more grown-up taste twist: cappuccino truffles. Simply replace the cocoa mix with cappuccino mix or a tablespoon of decaffeinated coffee. You may even want to try rolling the truffles in chopped nuts or colorful candy sprinkles.

EDIBLE VALENTINE CARDS
Here are fun-n-fancy treats for a special day.

Whatcha Need: You'll need paper plates, plastic knives, graham crackers, pink or white canned icing, candy conversation hearts, small cinnamon candy hearts, raisins, chocolate chips, candy sprinkles, and peanuts.

Whatcha Know!

Older kids may enjoy using graham crackers to assemble festive Valentine's Day gingerbread houses!

Whatcha Do: Hand each person a paper plate and two graham crackers (the double kind so the cards are large enough to easily decorate). Let kids spread canned icing on their graham crackers. Then, in the center of the edible cards, have kids place conversation hearts to spell out messages to their special Valentines. Place cinnamon candies or candy sprinkles around the edges and finish by adding raisins, peanuts, or chocolate chips. For a whole church idea, let kids set up a table with bowls of ingredients, plastic knives, and plenty of graham crackers and canned icing. After the service, invite church members to make a sweet treat to eat or to give to someone.

SPRING-BOARD
A handy springtime memo keeper for Mom.

Whatcha Need: You'll need small self-adhesive note pads (one per child), bendable wire, scissors, small pencils, bright foam board, markers, tape, and ½-inch wide ribbon.

Whatcha Do: Cut the foam board into 6-inch squares, the ribbon into 8-inch lengths, and the wire into 12-inch lengths. Hand each child a foam-board square, a small self-adhesive note pad, a pencil, a piece of ribbon, and a length of wire. Have kids turn their squares to make kite shapes and use markers to decorate the foam board. To assemble each kite, wrap wire around and around a pencil, then slide it off of the pencil and gently pull to make a stretched-out spring. Tape the spring at the bottom point of the kite. Stick the pencil between the spring coils to hold it in place. Tape the ribbon in a loop at the top of the kite for hanging. Stick a self-adhesive notepad to the center of the kite. Explain to kids that as notes are written they can be stuck around the edges of the kites. If these cute kites are to used as Mother's Day gifts, be sure to have kids write "thank you, Mom" notes on a couple pieces of note-pad paper and to stick them to the kites.

For a colorful springtime bulletin-board display, make your kites the same way, but omit the note pads and the pencils in the coils. Instead, tie 4-inch lengths of ribbon to the coils for kite tails. Color and cut out pictures from Bible-story coloring books and glue them to the centers of the kites. Use glitter, sequins, and plastic jewels for sparkling embellishments. Finally, add a title board to your display that says, "Fly high with God's Word!"

STRAWBERRY STONES
Yummy surprise buns make perfect Easter treats.

Whatcha Need: You'll need a cookie sheet, refrigerator biscuits, tube icing, strawberries, and mini jelly beans. You'll also need access to an oven or a large toaster oven.

Whatcha Do: Make sure kids' hands are clean, then hand each person a refrigerator biscuit. Have kids knead the dough into balls or "stones," then poke a jelly bean into the center of each dough stone. Place the dough stones on a cookie sheet and bake the biscuits according to the package directions or until they're golden brown. Cool the treats, then squirt icing crosses on the tops of the buns. Place a strawberry in the center of each cross. Remind kids that a large stone sealed the tomb where Jesus lay after his death on the cross. Point out that the tomb held a sweet secret—and that after three days, that sweet secret was revealed when the stone was rolled away and the tomb was opened. Remind kids how Jesus has conquered death and been resurrected to new life and that through Jesus' love and forgiveness we are invited to share in the sweetness of eternal life with God, too!

EASTER STORY BASKET
A basket to help retell the story of the first Easter.

Whatcha Need: You'll need small plastic baskets (one per person), permanent markers, jelly beans, and the following items for each child: a small stone, four plastic pull-apart Easter eggs, a small cross (or paper to make one), and three small nails.

Whatcha Do: Let kids use permanent markers to decorate their small baskets and pull-apart eggs. Number the eggs one to four. (Have kids make paper crosses if they need to at this time.) As they work, encourage kids to retell the story of the first Easter by asking them questions such as:
- *What did Jesus teach us about serving at the Last Supper?*
- *Why did Jesus pray before he was arrested in the garden?*
- *Why was Jesus hung on the cross?*
- *What happened on the morning of the third day after Jesus' death?*

After the eggs and baskets are finished, have kids add items to their eggs as you tell them what each symbolizes:
- *Egg 1: The Cross.* (Place a cross and a black jelly bean in the first egg.) **Inside the first egg is a cross that reminds us how Jesus willingly carried and died on a cross to save us from eternal death, which is represented by the black jelly bean. Jesus endured the cross to forgive our sins so that we could be close to God.**

- **Egg 2: The Nails.** (Place three nails and a red jelly bean in the second egg.) **Inside the second egg are three nails that remind us how Jesus was nailed to the cross. Jesus suffered great pain and shed his blood** (red jelly bean) **to pay the price for our sins.**
- **Egg 3: The Stone.** (Place a small stone and a yellow jelly bean in the third egg.) **Inside the third egg is a small stone that symbolizes the huge stone that sealed the tomb where Jesus lay after his death on the cross. On the third morning after Jesus' death when the sun rose in the sky** (yellow jelly bean), **Jesus' friends came to his tomb and saw that the stone had been rolled away.**
- **Egg 4: JESUS IS RISEN!** (Place no object in the fourth egg.) **The fourth egg is empty to symbolize how Jesus was raised from death and how the tomb was found empty on that first Easter morning. Jesus was risen, just as he had promised. And just as he promises us, we will have eternal life if we accept Jesus into our hearts and lives!**

Close by reading aloud Matthew 28:6 and offering a prayer of thanks for Jesus' forgiveness of our sins and his gift of eternal life. Challenge kids to use their storytelling eggs to retell the story of the first Easter to their families and friends.

SILVER CHIMES

Unusual wind chimes that are loads of fun to make!

Whatcha Need: You'll need fishing line, wire or plastic clothes hangers, scissors, and lots of old silver flatware (available at thrift stores or garage sales).

Whatcha Do: Ask kids to tell about wind chimes they've seen. Explain that, even though the wind is invisible, we "see" what it does through the ways wind chimes move and through the sounds they make. Point out that we "see" the Holy Spirit through all he does for us, too. Have kids cut varying lengths of fishing line. Then show kids how to tie one end of the fishing line to the handles of flatware and the other end to clothes hangers to make mobiles. When the wind blows, the flatware moves and clinks together with delightful sounds! Tell kids to hang their wind chimes in breezy windows, on porches, or in trees as reminders of how the Holy Spirit moves in our lives as we see all he does through us.

SUMMERTIME SMOOTHIES

Sip these cool smoothies on a sizzling day.

Whatcha Need: You'll need frozen strawberries, vanilla ice cream, chilled apple juice, plastic drinking straws, a mixing spoon, and self-sealing sandwich bags.

Whatcha Do: For each smoothie, place one or two spoonfuls of vanilla ice cream in a self-sealing sandwich bag. Add one spoonful of frozen strawberries, then fill the bag half full of chilled apple juice. Seal the bag tightly and gently squeeze the contents to mix them. When the ice cream, juice, and berries are smooth, open one edge of the sandwich bag and slide in a plastic drinking straw.

Try one of these recipes for more smoothie fun.
- Mix ice cream, peanut butter, and chocolate syrup in a sandwich bag.
- In a sandwich bag, blend ripe bananas, coconut, and vanilla yogurt.
- Mix vanilla ice cream, oatmeal, butterscotch syrup, and mini chocolate chips in a sandwich bag and invite kids to enjoy!

 # NO WATER WASTE
Handy garden helpers water plants without waste.

Whatcha Need: You'll need 4-inch nails, clear plastic soda bottles (remove labels), a knife, and paint pens.

Whatcha Do: Before class, cut the top third from the plastic soda bottles using a knife. Gather kids and remind them that God created the world for us to enjoy and live in responsibly. Point out that we want to be good stewards of all God has given us and to be careful not to waste the pure things we need to live, such as air and water. Explain that you'll be making special water tubes to water plants and flowers without waste. Hand each person a plastic soda bottle and nail. Show kids how to poke holes around the bottom portion of the bottles. Poke six to ten holes in the bottles. Use paint pens to decorate the soda bottles with designs such as flowers, plants, sunshine, or even rainbows and rain clouds. After the paints dry, show kids how the bottles can be set beside the base of plants or flowers, then filled with water from a pitcher. The water will slowly drip and seep out of the bottle and soak into the ground where the plants need water the most. These make great gifts and can be used to water the flowers around the church!

> ## Whatcha Know!
>
> Let kids use various sizes of plastic bottles, including milk jugs and plastic jars, to make watering systems for various sizes of plants and shrubs. Nest the containers in the milk jugs for simple storage.

 # DAD'S DAY KEY RING
A nifty gift dads will appreciate.

Whatcha Need: You'll need satin cord, round key-ring hoops (from a craft store), pony beads, scissors, and fine-tipped permanent markers. (Hint: If you can't find round key rings, use large safety pins.)

Whatcha Do: Cut satin cord into a 15-inch length for each person. Show kids how to tie their cords half-hitch style to the key ring hoops. (To make a half-hitch knot, hold the loop under the key ring and pull the ends of the cord up and over the key ring and down through the loop. Pull tightly to secure the hitch.) Invite kids to choose six pony beads and, using the fine-tipped permanent markers, write the word "DAD" (one letter per bead) and draw small hearts on the other three beads. String both cords on the key ring through one of the heart beads. Separate the cords, then string the left cord through a "D" bead. String the right cord through the other "D" bead. Join the cords and string on the other two heart beads. Making sure the bottom heart beads are positioned snuggly against the two "D" beads, tie a knot under the bottom heart bead. Insert the "A" bead between the two "D" beads. (The tension will hold the "A" beads securely in place!)

For a simpler version of the same key ring, slide three beads through the ends of both cords and tie a knot to hold them in place. Use permanent markers to spell the word "DAD" (one letter per bead) going down the cords. Use the same method and let kids spell other words or join other shapes to make unique messages.

POP-UP GARDEN

A scented garden with favorite springtime flowers.

Whatcha Need: You'll need flower stickers, colored construction paper, perfume (or lilac oil), cotton swabs, glue, scissors, and markers.

Whatcha Do: Practice folding and cutting a couple of these gardens so you're familiar with the steps. Lead kids through each step as follows.

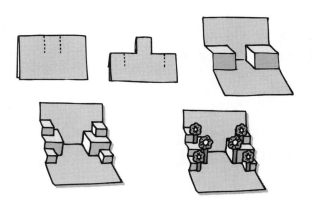

Step 1: Fold a piece of construction paper in half, then cut two short lines near the middle of the fold.

Step 2: Fold the two outside flaps forward, but do not fold the middle flap. Unfold the flaps.

Step 3: Open the paper. Push the two flaps forward to form two "steps."

Step 4: Refold the paper, and cut two short lines through the folded flaps on the sides. Fold the outside flaps that you just cut as you did in step 2. Unfold the flaps.

Step 5: Open the paper. Push the two flaps forward to form four small "steps" beside the two larger ones (as you did in step 3).

Step 6: Cut green construction-paper stems and glue them to the fronts of the steps, then add flower stickers to the stems. Use cotton swabs to spread a little perfume (or lilac oil) on the flowers. Finally, use markers to write God give us flowers..." across the top portion of the paper above the garden and "God gives us springtime!" across the bottom of the garden.

AWESOME ORGANIZATION

Clever clues, helpful hints,
tons of tips, and more make
this section an invaluable
classroom resource!

Who can resist a hint, tip, or shortcut to increase the learning fun and decrease the work? This section is loaded with clever helps to lighten your load. From the instant games and crafts boxes to reproducible charts and checklists, you'll discover something useful for every area of classroom management. Read through these teacher-tested tips 'n hints, then go ahead and use 'em now!

 Make nifty **pencil holders** to keep markers or pencils right at kids' fingertips. Punch holes in the top edges of small plastic cups and thread yarn or cord through the holes. Tie the cord to backs, legs, or arms of chairs. Personalize the cups by having kids decorate them using paint pens or permanent markers. Be sure to include your names! Send the cups home at the end of the year.

 Make a **table organizer** for craft and writing supplies. Cut the tops off of four milk cartons and glue them together (two rows of two) with craft glue. Use duct tape or colored vinyl tape to reinforce the top edges and base. Now you're ready to organize your supplies! Use the cartons to hold pencils, pens, markers, scissors, glue, crayons, or other supplies you use often. (Make the organizer larger by simply adding more cartons.)

Here's a helpful hint for storing **markers.** Take a plastic margarine tub and fill it with 3 inches of plaster of Paris. While the plaster is still damp, insert markers (cap down) with about three-quarters of the cap in the plaster, then let the plaster harden. When it's dry, simply pull out the markers as needed and the caps stay in place without being lost! Purchase the same kind of markers each time you replace them and simply reuse the caps in the plaster tub.

 Speaking of **crayons** … have you ever had to remove crayon or marker stains from tables, counters, or clothing? Try rubbing white toothpaste on the spot, then washing it with warm, soapy water.

 At the beginning of the year, let each child write his name on a new craft stick, then place the craft sticks in a can or decorative gift sack. Use the **name sticks** to call on kids, choose leaders, find classroom helpers, and much more!

 Ever have regular marker stains on your white, dry-erase board? A quick **cleaning solution** is to use the correct type of dry-erase marker to write over the stain. This breaks down the permanent ink, and the whole mess wipes away! (You can also use a bit of nonaerosol hair spray to do the trick!)

A great way to keep classroom tables clean is to cover them with **plastic tablecloths** or triple sheets of **butcher paper** when children are working with glue, markers, or paint. Layers of butcher paper can simply be peeled away for cleaning in a snap. Plastic tablecloths can be attached under the table with self-adhesive hook-and-loop fasteners or double-sided tape. Check discount stores for bargains on festive tablecloths after holidays!

A little **positive reinforcement** goes a long way! Consider ordering printed address labels that contain messages for kids. Suggested messages might include "Great job! You're tops!" "I'm glad you were here today!" and "Jesus loves you—so do I!"

Baby wipes are excellent for cleaning hands after messy crafts or before snacks. They're also super for tidying up table tops, wiping dry-erase boards, and even cleaning small spills on the carpet.

Keep scissors, rulers, crayon boxes, or other craft items securely in one place by attaching **self-adhesive hook-and-loop fasteners** to the items and to an old cookie sheet or TV tray. The tray can be carried from table to table or table to shelf without items tumbling off.

Here's a new twist to an old idea. Instead of using messy ink pads when doing **thumb prints** for craft projects, use chocolate syrup! Kids don't mind licking their fingers after projects to clean up the "stains."

Let kids make cool **rainbow crayons** by gathering up the snubs and stubs of crayons you already have (or can bring from home). Remove the paper from the crayons, then place the pieces in muffin pans lined with aluminum foil. Melt the crayons in a 250-degree oven for about five minutes. (Watch carefully to avoid burning the wax.) You may need to stir the wax as it melts. When the crayons are melted, cool them for several hours, then peel off the foil. (Hint: Keep black and brown by themselves.)

Are you always short of **paintbrushes**? Try making inexpensive brushes by clipping small pieces of sponge to hinge-style clothespins. Cutting the sponges into various shapes makes interesting brush strokes!

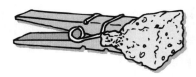

Dried glue often clogs the tips of glue bottles. Spray **nonstick cooking spray** on the insides of the orange glue caps for a slick-n-quick remedy!

Markers dry up easily when kids forget to replace the caps or when the markers sit over a few weeks without being used. To reactivate ink, simply dunk the markers (without the caps) in a cup of water for a few minutes. It works great, and kids love to see the water change colors.

 When mixing **powdered tempera paint,** use one part liquid hand or dish soap and three parts water. This makes cleanup much easier and helps with the laundry in case kids spill paint on their clothes. (You many also want to try keeping tempera paints in empty shampoo bottles for easy storage and pouring!)

 Make **aprons** in a snap by stapling several layers of paper toweling to 1-by-24-inch lengths of colorful ribbon. Simply tear off paper towels as they become messy or sticky.

 To keep **chalkboards** clean, use a facial tissue that has lanolin or hand lotion on it. Wrap the tissue around the eraser, then erase the board. You'll rarely have to wash the board because the bit of oil makes it look like new and helps prevent bits of dust from clinging to the board.

 Another **chalkboard** tip eliminates drippy cloths and soggy sponges while keeping black-boards looking like new! Place a drop of lemon oil on a clean washcloth and slide the cloth in a self-sealing sandwich bag. Leave the cloth in the bag overnight so the oil soaks into the cloth. Simply erase the chalkboard as usual, then wipe over the board using the cloth.

 Keep **posters** on your wall all year long by using a bit of hot glue in the corners. Hot glue won't harm the poster or your wall and keeps displays and posters from sliding off the walls each week.

 To keep posters, wall hangings, and bulletin boards looking new and unbent, store them in **plastic trash bags,** then clip them to pants hangers and hang them in a closet. (Be sure to add a label to each bag to save time in finding your displays.)

 Use an **egg carton** to hold a dozen markers. Turn the carton upside down, poke a hole in each egg cup, and cover the bottom (which was the egg carton top) with duct tape so the markers won't fall through the holes.

Make several photocopies of the following **checklists,** charts, and forms. Keep them in folders and pull them out to use in an instant.

 BEST-FOR-LAST TIPS:
1. Treat every child with respect.
2. Develop and keep a sense of humor.
3. Be flexible.
4. Meet 'n greet kids with a smile and a hug.
5. Pray for your kids each day.

SHOPPING SUPPLY LIST

Classroom Supplies

- ❏ chalk
- ❏ construction paper
- ❏ crayons
- ❏ drawing paper
- ❏ glue or paste
- ❏ markers

- ❏ newsprint
- ❏ paintbrushes
- ❏ paints
- ❏ pencils
- ❏ scissors

Party Supplies

- ❏ balloons
- ❏ crepe paper
- ❏ decorations

_____

_____

_____

_____

- ❏ favors
- ❏ flatware
- ❏ invitations
- ❏ napkins

- ❏ paper cups
- ❏ paper plates
- ❏ paper towels

Food Items

_____

_____

_____

_____

Miscellaneous Items

_____

_____

_____

_____

CLASS LIST

YEAR: _____

LEADER: _____ PHONE: _____

Child's name	Address	Phone	Birthday	Parent/Guardian

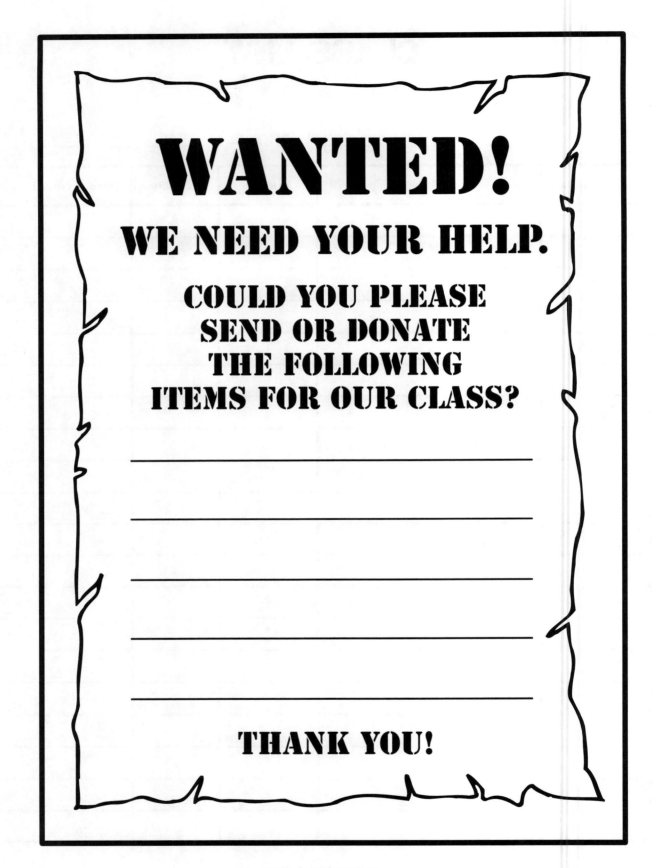

WANTED!

WE NEED YOUR HELP.

COULD YOU PLEASE
SEND OR DONATE
THE FOLLOWING
ITEMS FOR OUR CLASS?

_____

_____

_____

_____

_____

THANK YOU!

MORE

SOS FOR THE SUBSTITUTE

Safe (and sane!) activities for substitute teachers and spur-of-the-moment volunteers!

A Bit of Background

Few things in life are as rare to find and difficult to keep as substitute teachers and spur-of-the-moment volunteers! Every children's worker and leader knows the frustration of trying to fine someone to take his place in the event of illness or conflicting schedules. Trying to convince someone there's plenty of activities to keep kids actively involved is almost impossible! Besides, what if your plans aren't written down for someone to follow at the last moment? It can be a recipe for disaster! But once you've assembled the awesome substitute folder included in this section of *More 200+ Activities for Children's Ministry,* you'll feel confident that whoever takes your place will be equipped and ready to offer kids lively activities and learning at a moment's notice. Simply follow the instructions in this section to make an invaluable tool for your classroom to use when you need help—and a helping hand! Here are a few additional hints to help you be prepared!

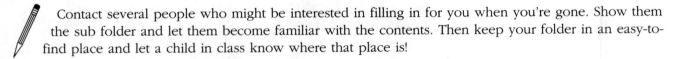

Contact several people who might be interested in filling in for you when you're gone. Show them the sub folder and let them become familiar with the contents. Then keep your folder in an easy-to-find place and let a child in class know where that place is!

Consider decorating a small box with festive gift wrap. In it, place plastic knives, peanut butter and crackers (impromptu snacks), small wrapped candies (special treat or reward), a tennis ball (for quick games), and a package of balloons (quick games or craft activities). Place your sub folder on top of the other items, and you're ready for anything!

Be sure to keep a stash of fun-to-read Bible storybooks on hand, along with a pile of inexpensive Bible-story coloring books and crayons. These items always help out in a pinch and keep kids occupied in enjoyable ways.

Change the items in your sub folder if you've been absent several times during the year. New riddles, jokes, crafts, and games are available in the original *200+ Activities for Children's Ministry*—along with a different section for the substitute teacher!

CONTENTS OF
THE SOS FOLDER

❑ class list
❑ Bible-trivia cards
❑ Bible jokes-n-riddles cards
❑ two reproducible coloring pages
❑ two reproducible Scripture puzzles

❑ one or two Bible storybooks
❑ Quick Games page
❑ Quick Crafts page
❑ general information page
❑ schedule page

SUPPLIES FOR ASSEMBLING
THE SOS FOLDER

You'll need a solid-colored file folder or notebook with pockets, construction paper, permanent markers, several small envelopes, a stapler, tape, a Bible coloring book and a puzzle book, small Bible storybooks, and the photocopies listed in the directions that follow.

ASSEMBLING THE SOS FOLDER

1. Photocopy the Class List from page 95. Fill in the information, then highlight the names of several children you feel would be helpful to a substitute leader. Be sure to indicate on the list what the highlighted names signify! Staple the Class List to the top edge of the folder front.

2. Make a photocopy of the Our Schedule from page 101. Fill in the blanks in general categories such as Bible-story time, devotion time, snack time, and so on. Staple this page over the top of the Class List so it will lift up to reveal the list underneath.

3. Photocopy on colored paper the Bible Trivia cards and the Bible Jokes & Riddles cards from page 102. Cut apart the cards and store them in separate envelopes. Tape the envelopes, open sides facing out to the fronts of the inside pockets, then label the envelopes as in the illustration on page 100.

4. Place thin-bound Bible storybooks in the pocket on the left side. Be sure the books are thin and small enough to fit neatly in the folder.

5. Make one photocopy each of two pictures from a Bible coloring book. Turn these pages into color-by-number pages by numbering the coloring spaces and adding a color-coded key on the page. Use these "master copies" with notes to "photocopy as needed." You may wish to run off a set for your kids and have them in the folder. Do the same for two pages from a Scripture puzzle book. Keep the original copy in the pocket on the right side of the folder.

6. Make one photocopy each of the Quick Games page (page 103) and the Quick Crafts page (page 104). Keep these idea pages in the right-side pocket.

7. Photocopy the general information sheet from page 105. Fill out the information and draw a simple map indicating the fire-escape route you'd take for your class. Staple this important page to the back cover of the folder.

Our Schedule

FROM (time)	TO (time)	ACTIVITY/LESSON

BIBLE TRIVIA

Who went up by a whirlwind into heaven?

(Elijah)

What youth killed a lion and a bear while tending his father's sheep?

(David)

What did John the Baptist eat?

(locusts and honey)

Who climbed a sycamore tree to see Jesus?

(Zacchaeus)

Who was turned into a pillar of salt?

(Lot's wife)

What are the names of the four Gospels?

(Matthew, Mark, Luke, John)

Which leader commanded the sun to stand still?

(Joshua)

How many stones did David gather before he killed Goliath?

(five)

Who was the female judge of Israel?

(Deborah)

What animal spoke to Balaam?

(a donkey)

What was the musical instrument played by David?

(the harp or lyre)

How many books are in the Bible?

(66: 39 Old Testament and 27 New Testament)

BIBLE JOKES & RIDDLES

What did the chewing gum say to the shepherd's sandals?

(I'm stuck on you!)

After spitting out Jonah, why did the whale cross the road?

(to get to the other tide)

Which fish go to heaven when they die?

(angelfish)

How can you make seven even?

(just take away the letter S)

Who was the greatest comedian in the Bible?

(Samson, because he brought the house down)

What kind of lights were on the ark?

(floodlights)

Which insect loves church?

(the praying mantis!)

Did all the animals on the ark come in pairs (pears)?

(no, the worms came in apples)

What was Boaz before he married Ruth?

(Ruthless)

Who was in trouble for stealing the soap in the bathroom?

(the robber ducky)

What is the best way to get to heaven?

(You turn right and go straight.)

Who was known as a mathematician in the Bible?

(Moses, because he wrote the book of Numbers)

QUICK GAMES

Make Me Laugh—Choose one player to be the Laugh Master and hand him a sheet of paper. Position the Laugh Master at one end of the room and everyone else at the opposite end. Tell kids the Laugh Master will toss the sheet of paper in the air. As the paper flutters down, kids are to laugh out loud and walk heel-to-toe forward but must freeze and stop laughing when the paper touches the floor. If the Laugh Master sees anyone moving or giggling, that player must return to the starting place and begin again. The first person to tap the Laugh Master becomes the next Laugh Master.

Picture Puzzler—Have kids form pairs or trios and hand each small group a sheet of white paper and markers. Assign a different verse for each team to write on its paper, then have teams draw pictures to illustrate the verses. Cut the pages into six large puzzle pieces, then place the pieces in a bag or basket. Hide the pieces around the room, then let teams go on a puzzle hunt. Have each team find six pieces and begin assembling a verse. Have them run back and forth between other teams switching pieces until one team wins by completing a puzzle. Read that puzzle aloud and set the pieces aside. Scramble the other pieces and hide them again. Repeat the game until all of the verses have been assembled.

Volloon Ball—Inflate and tie off a balloon. Mark a square on the floor using masking tape. Place an X in the square going from corner to corner. Form four teams and have each team stand in one section of the square. Begin volleying the balloon back and forth. Each time the balloon goes out of bounds or touches the floor, the team who last touched the balloon sores one point against them. Play for ten minutes. The winner is the team with the least amount of points. (Play a variation where each time the ball is volleyed, you name a different book of the Bible!)

Do, Re, Mi!—Seat kids in a circle. Choose one person to be It and have him sit in the center of the circle. The player in the center begins by saying, "Do, Re, Mi—Do, Re, Mi…" The child points to someone in the circle as he says either "Do," "Re," or "Me." If the child says "Do," the person pointed to says the name of the person to her right. If he says "Re," the person pointed to says the name of the person on her left. And if "It" calls "Mi," the person pointed to says her own name. If the person pointed to says a wrong name, everyone scrambles to change places in the circle. While everyone is changing places, the child who is It tags another player to take his place in the center of the circle. (If kids already know each other's names well, assign new directions for "Do, "Re," and "Mi," such as naming a fruit on "Do," a vegetable on "Re," and a car type on "Mi." If someone misses, exchange places.)

QUICK CRAFTS

✂ **Hug-Me's**—Cut construction paper into 3-by-22-inch strips. (You may have to cut several shorter strips and tape them together to make one long strip.) Trace your hands on colored paper, then cut out the paper hands. Tape or glue the paper hands to the ends of the long paper strips. Write "Love each other as I have loved you—John 15:12" one one palm and "Be devoted to one another in brotherly love—Romans 12:10" on the other. Use the hug-me's to wrap yourselves in hugs, then wrap someone else in a big hug. Sing "Jesus Loves Me" and wrap yourself in hugs each time you sing the word "loves."

✂ **Envelope Puppets**—Hand out envelopes and have kids lick and seal them. Carefully cut widthwise through one layer of the envelope on the side with the sealed flap (don't cut lengthwise). Fold the envelope in half, then slide your hands in the two pockets on either side of the cut. Open and close your fingers to make the puppets "talk." Color the puppets and add facial features. Glue or tape strips of colored paper on for hair. Use your hand puppets to present and retell your favorite Bible stories.

✂ **Fanciful Flowerpots**—Hand each person a paper or foam cup. Cover the cups with short pieces of masking tape, mosaic style. Be sure the entire outside of each cup is covered with pieces of masking tape. Use crayons to color over the tape, making sure you color over the seams of the tape where the crayon will be darker and look beautiful! Use many colors and color the entire outsides of the cups. Kids can use potting soil and seeds at home to plant their pots or have kids make paper flowers to tape to the inside edges of the pots. Make flowers using rolled-paper stems and paper flower tops. Read aloud Matthew 6:28, 29, then have kids use markers to write "See how the lilies of the field grow" on their pots or flowers.

✂ **Wristlets**—Kids love making these fun-to-wear bracelets! Begin by cutting ½-by-½-inch pieces of colored paper. Roll the pieces into small tubes and tape the seams. Make several of these colored "beads." Add dots or stripes using fine-tipped markers or pens. Thread the beads onto paper clips, then link the paper clips together to form a chain. When the chain is long enough to go around wrists, add a few more clips to allow the bracelet to slip over your hands. You may wish to have kids each make two wristlets—one to wear and one to share!

GENERAL INFORMATION

Minister: _____

Other Leader: _____

CE Director: _____

Other helpful information: _____

_____

_____

_____

FIRE-ESCAPE ROUTE

ZIB-ZUB

PRAYER MODELS

Meet and greet	Dear loving and powerful God,
Require and desire	Please help me grow closer to you.
Confession	Forgive my hurtful words and selfish things I do.
Intercession	Please help me help others to know you, too.
Thank-you	Thank you, dear Father—I love you! Amen.

Meet and greet	Dear loving and powerful God,
Require and desire	Please help me grow closer to you.
Confession	Forgive my hurtful words and selfish things I do.
Intercession	Please help me help others to know you, too.
Thank-you	Thank you, dear Father—I love you! Amen.

Meet and greet	Dear loving and powerful God,
Require and desire	Please help me grow closer to you.
Confession	Forgive my hurtful words and selfish things I do.
Intercession	Please help me help others to know you, too.
Thank-you	Thank you, dear Father—I love you! Amen.

Meet and greet	Dear loving and powerful God,
Require and desire	Please help me grow closer to you.
Confession	Forgive my hurtful words and selfish things I do.
Intercession	Please help me help others to know you, too.
Thank-you	Thank you, dear Father—I love you! Amen.

Meet and greet	Dear loving and powerful God,
Require and desire	Please help me grow closer to you.
Confession	Forgive my hurtful words and selfish things I do.
Intercession	Please help me help others to know you, too.
Thank-you	Thank you, dear Father—I love you! Amen.

ACTIVITY INDEX

MORE CREATIVE CRAFTS

MORE GREAT GAMES

MORE GOODIES GALORE

MORE PRAYER & WORSHIP

MORE DEVOTIONS & OBJECT LESSONS

MORE SUPER SEASONALS